Earnings Capacity, Poverty, and Inequality

This is a volume in the

Institute for Research on Poverty Monograph Series

A complete list of titles in this series appears at the end of this volume.

Earnings Capacity, Poverty, and Inequality

Irwin Garfinkel

The University of Wisconsin—Madison
Madison, Wisconsin

Robert H. Haveman

The University of Wisconsin—Madison
Madison, Wisconsin

With the Assistance of
David Betson
U.S. Department of Health,
Education, and Welfare
Washington, D.C.

Academic Press
New York   San Francisco   London
A Subsidiary of Harcourt Brace Jovanovich, Publishers

This book is one of a series sponsored by the Institute for Research on Poverty of the University of Wisconsin pursuant to the provisions of the Economic Opportunity Act of 1964.

ACADEMIC PRESS, INC.
111 Fifth Avenue, New York, New York 10003

United Kingdom Edition published by
ACADEMIC PRESS, INC. (LONDON) LTD.
24/28 Oval Road, London NW1

Library of Congress Cataloging in Publication Data

Garfinkel, Irwin.
    Earnings capacity, poverty, and inequality.

    Bibliography: p.
        1.   Income distribution—United States.
2.   Poverty.   I.   Haveman, Robert H., joint author.
II.   Title.
HC110.I5G37   339.2   77-80784
ISBN 0-12-275850-1

PRINTED IN THE UNITED STATES OF AMERICA

The Institute for Research on Poverty is a national center for research established at the University of Wisconsin in 1966 by a grant from the Office of Economic Opportunity. Its primary objective is to foster basic, multidisciplinary research into the nature and causes of poverty and means to combat it.

In addition to increasing the basic knowledge from which policies aimed at the elimination of poverty can be shaped, the Institute strives to carry analysis beyond the formulation and testing of fundamental generalizations to the development and assessment of relevant policy alternatives.

The Institute endeavors to bring together scholars of the highest caliber whose primary research efforts are focused on the problem of poverty, the distribution of income, and the analysis and evaluation of social policy, offering staff members wide opportunity for interchange of ideas, maximum freedom for research into basic questions about poverty and social policy, and dissemination of their findings.

Contents

Foreword

What is the case for using "earnings capacity" as a measure of a family's economic status? Is this measure superior to other indicators such as annual money income, which is the standard measure? These are the questions examined by Professors Garfinkel and Haveman, the present Director and a former Director, respectively, of the Institute for Research on Poverty. They discuss the weaknesses of the current income measure of economic status, argue that the earnings capacity concept is a superior measure for many purposes, and develop empirical estimates of individual and family earnings capacity. They employ these estimates in identifying the composition of the poor population, in evaluating the effectiveness of alternative income-support programs in aiding those with the lowest economic position, in appraising how various groups utilize their earnings capacity, and in measuring the magnitude of the effect on black incomes of labor market discrimination.

The authors define earnings capacity as the amount of money an adult would receive if he or she worked 2000 hours per year in the market at his or her level of capability and if, at the same time, all that person's property were earning a normal money income. A family's earnings capacity is assessed by summing the property income and the potential earnings of the head and spouse in the family.

Each of the chapters contains interesting and, in some cases, controversial findings. For example, the authors attribute nearly 80 percent of income inequality to inequality in the distribution of earnings capacity; only 20 percent is accounted for by the differential use of capacity among families. Also, earnings capacity poverty is found to be more common than money income poverty for blacks, large families, and families with working wives. In their analysis of the target efficiency of alternative transfer program options, Garfinkel and Haveman find that negative income tax programs do not target their benefits on the earnings-capacity poor much better than do alternative income maintenance programs, such as wage rate or earnings subsidies or even children's allowances. Finally, it is estimated that much of the relatively low earnings of blacks is due to labor market discrimination, as opposed to differences between blacks and whites in socioeconomic characteristics (age, education, location) or in tastes for income versus leisure.

Perhaps the most controversial aspect of the measure is that a family could be called earnings-capacity poor or nonpoor without reference to either its actual earnings or its total money income. This raises a number of questions which are not resolved in this volume. For example, if earnings capacity is the best measure of economic status, would it be more appropriate to design policies to correct for deficiencies in earnings capacity rather than for deficiencies in actual earnings? This would be consistent with devoting less attention to cash transfers and more to policies designed to alter both the supply (education and training programs) and demand (antidiscrimination and job creation policies) sides of the labor market so as to modify differences in the capacity to earn.

Similarly, should benefits in transfer programs be conditioned on earnings capacity rather than current income? Because of incentives to pursue antisocial behavior associated with benefits conditioned upon actual earnings, some have searched for ways to relate benefits more closely to difficult-to-alter personal characteristics—such as those that form the basis of earnings capacity. The concept of relating benefits to earnings capacity is reminiscent of taxation according to a person's "faculty" to earn, as practiced in colonial New England, and is related to Jan Tinbergen's suggestion that psychologists and economists work toward developing a measure of permanent capabilities on which tax and transfer policy could focus. Such a notion, of course, also serves as the basis of categorical, means-tested public assistance. This approach is quite different from the philosophy of the ideal, noncategorical negative income tax whose benefits are conditioned only by actual earnings and family size.

This study contributes to the long tradition of research designed to improve the measurement of economic status and inequality, a tradition that has experienced a major increase in interest in the last decade. In addition to this volume, a number of other recent and forthcoming Institute work has explored or made use of alternative measures of economic status and related definitions of poverty: Robert D. Plotnick and Felicity Skidmore, *Progress Against Poverty: A Review of the 1964–1974 Decade* (1975); Timothy Smeeding, "Measuring the Economic Welfare of Low Income Households and the Antipoverty Effectiveness of Cash and Non-Cash Transfer Programs" (Ph.D. dissertation, University of Wisconson—Madison, 1975); Michael K. Taussig and Sheldon Danziger, *Conference on the Trend in Income Inequality in the U.S.,* Special Report 11 (1977); Marilyn Moon, *The Measurement of Economic Welfare: Its Application to the Aged* (1977); and Marilyn Moon and Eugene Smolensky (Eds.), *Improving Measures of Economic Well-Being* (1977).

By criticizing the standard approach to measuring economic position and inequality, and suggesting an alternative to it, the volume fits what Alice Rivlin has termed "forensic social science." Because such an approach does not provide the sorts of arguments and evidence present in a legal brief for the opposition the reader will need to test the authors' arguments as he goes along. Is earnings capacity too subjective a concept to serve as the basis for policymaking? Can conditions of disability and unemployability be adequately measured in the earnings capacity concept? For what sorts of policy issues is a longer term indicator of economic status, such as earnings capacity, more appropriate than an indicator of current need, such as annual money income? The alert and questioning reader will find this study a challenging one that stimulates reexamination of both social policy goals and social practices.

Robert Lampman
Department of Economics
University of Wisconsin—Madison
Madison, Wisconsin

Preface

The decision to undertake this study was rooted in the judgment that measures of economic status based on current income are likely to be misleading for policy purposes. For example, evaluators of income support programs were and still are giving low marks to programs that provide benefits to families with incomes above the poverty level. Yet, because the official poverty line is based on a money income measure, it may be that the only difference between a family officially classified as poor and an equivalent family classified as nonpoor may be that the latter family has a stronger taste for income relative to leisure and housework. The wife in the second family may work, while the wife in the first family may not. Is it correct to say that the latter family is less poor than the former? We would argue that this income difference between the two families is attributable to differences in tastes and not to fundamental differences in structure and income-earning capacities.

To correct some of the shortcomings of the current income measure—in particular, its dependence on relative tastes for income and leisure and to a lesser extent its transitory nature—we have defined an alternative measure of economic position. We call this measure "earnings capacity" because it indicates the amount of income that a household could generate if the household's capabilities were fully used. On the basis of this definition, we have estimated the earnings capacity of a national sample of American households.

Then, measuring poverty in terms of both earnings capacity and current income, we examine how effective various income support programs—negative income taxes, wage and earnings subsidies, and children's allowances—are in targeting their benefits on the poor.

We also use the earnings capacity measure to investigate a number of other questions of concern to both scholars and policymakers. How extensively do various population groups—married versus single, black versus white, well-to-do versus low income—use their earnings capacity, and how much does this variation in earnings capacity contribute to economic inequality? Taking account of differences in earnings capacity and its use, how much of the black-white earnings capacity disparity is due to labor market discrimination? And how does such discrimination affect the distribution of income?

The study presented in this volume, then, has consequences for both research and policy. We view it as one step in the development and application of a new measure of economic status that avoids some of the pitfalls of the current income measure. Hence, in the last chapter, we present a research agenda proposing logical future steps for the extension of the earnings capacity concept.

We are indebted to numerous people who have assisted us in this study, but to none more than David Betson, now of the U.S. Department of Health, Education, and Welfare. He worked closely with both of us throughout the study, and is responsible for nearly all of the computer work that underlies the analysis. His role in both the conceptual and applied sections of Chapters 5 and 6 was that of a full collaborator, and his insights in several discussions kept us from making serious errors. Nancy Schofield and Nancy Williamson also contributed to the data preparation and calculations. Helpful comments on various sections were provided by participants in the Poverty Institute Seminar Series, who sat through at least four presentations of this material. John Bishop, Glen Cain, Arthur Goldberger, Stanley Masters, Eugene Smolensky, and Burton Weisbrod also furnished helpful comments and critiques. Two outside reviewers, Alan Blinder of Princeton University and Michael Taussig of Rutgers University, provided detailed and insightful critiques of an early draft of the entire volume. Chapter 4 appeared in a slightly different version as "Earnings Capacity, Economic Status, and Poverty," in *Journal of Human Resources* 12 (© 1977 by the Regents of the University of Wisconsin), pp. 49–70; Chapter 5 as "Earnings Capacity and the Target Efficiency of Alternative Transfer Programs," in *American Economic Review* 64 (© 1974 by the American Economic Association), pp. 196–204.

We would like to thank Camille Smith for her superb editing, which substantially improved the readability of the manuscript. For their efforts and patience we are most grateful to the Institute typists, especially Cathy Ersland, Wendy Haebig, and Marlene

Kundert. Finally, we acknowledge the invaluable administrative assistance provided by Beverly Neupert, which kept computer printouts and manuscript drafts well-ordered against overwhelming odds.

Irwin Garfinkel
Robert Haveman

1

Measuring Economic Status: The Concept of Earnings Capacity

It seems too bad, at a time when more attention is being given to problems of poverty and inequality, that we ... continue to collect and talk about data on dollar family income that are half after-transfers (they include some transfers and not others) and half adequate (they include only regular dollar flows), and half-baked because they take no account of how many people depend on the income or on how long they worked to get it.

James Morgan, 1968

Weaknesses in the measurement of the economic status of individuals and family units have long plagued both research and policy-making efforts. Traditionally, estimates of family and individual annual money income have served as proxies for economic status in studies of income distribution and poverty and in the making of social policy. However, few users of these estimates have been confident that estimated money income levels or changes in money income have adequately reflected the level of or changes in economic welfare. The measure based on money income excludes many components of economic status, and, in addition, its dependence on transitory phenomena reduces its reliability as an indicator of long-run economic position.

Over the years, economists have formulated numerous empirical measures of economic status to replace current money income. The study presented here is in the tradition of efforts to develop a measure of economic status that avoids the inadequacies of the current income indicator. The approach taken in most previous studies[1] has been to adjust the current income measure for a consumer unit so as to move toward a measure of potential real consumption. The procedure here is quite different. In this study, the index of economic status for a household unit is designed to measure the potential of the unit to generate an income stream if it were to use its physical and human capital to capacity. This measure is called *earnings capacity*. For many of the analyses employing this concept, the estimated value is adjusted by the welfare ratio technique to reflect the relationship of earnings capacity to household needs.[2]

For several conceptual reasons, earnings capacity is a more appealing measure of economic status than current money income. First, by focusing on using human and physical capital to capacity, this measure eliminates much of the effect of leisure–income preferences, an effect that is automatically built into measures based on current income. In such measures, a family unit with a strong taste for income will rank higher than an identical family with a weaker taste for income. For example, if the wife in one of two identical families chooses to work—or if the head chooses to be a craftsman rather than a farmer—that family will have a higher income and economic position than the other family. The concept of earnings capacity, on the other hand, focuses on the level of economic resources possessed by a household rather than on the household's taste for using these resources. Second, because the earnings capacity measure is closely related to the level of human and physical capital possessed by a household, it eliminates some of the transitory influences that affect both the current income of any unit and the degree of inequality in the distribution of money income. Earnings capacity, relatively free from transitory influences, lies closer to the concept of permanent or

---

[1] See Moon and Smolensky (1977) for a presentation of several of the studies, as well as a discussion of other approaches to the measurement of economic welfare.

[2] It should perhaps be emphasized that *earnings capacity* refers to potential income flows from both human and physical assets, while *earnings* typically refers to flows generated by only the former of these sources.

full income than does current money income. Finally, from a more sociological viewpoint, the measure of earnings capacity, by focusing on access to economic resources, seems to be more successful than measures of current money income in capturing a family's economic status.

Our objective in this study is to employ a measure of earnings capacity for the purpose of analyzing several research and public policy questions concerning economic status. These questions include the following: To what extent is inequality in the distribution of income attributable to differences in the taste for income versus leisure as opposed to differences in the capacity to earn income? Do individuals with low earnings capacity make more or less use of their ability to earn than do individuals with higher earnings capacity? Who are the poorest members of society, and what is the demographic composition of this group? How effectively would alternative income maintenance programs target their benefits on the poor if the poor were defined by earnings capacity rather than by current income? To what extent is the difference between the earnings of blacks and those of whites attributable to differences in earnings capacities rather than to racial discrimination in the labor market? The concept of earnings capacity and our measure of it enable us to address these questions.

Alternative Measures of Economic Status

Our formulation of earnings capacity is not the first effort to improve upon money income as a measure of economic status. One of the earliest such efforts was prompted by the discovery that current income was inadequate as a predictor of current consumption. Although the money income of a living unit rose and fell because of windfalls or the business cycle, the level of consumption remained rather stable, not strongly affected by such transitory or cylical changes in income. To explain these and other similar phenomena, the hypothesis that consumption in any period depends upon long-run or "permanent" income rather than current income was proposed and empirically tested. The work of Duesenberry (1949) and Friedman (1957) is prominent among these early contributions. This reformulation culminated in the work of Ando and Modigliani

(1963), who, within a lifetime utility maximization framework, defined what is now widely accepted as a comprehensive measure of economic position in any period. It is the individual's (or family's) optimal level of real consumption in a period, given the present value of the unit's total resources over its remaining lifetime. In this definition, consumption is defined as current outlays for nondurable goods and services plus the rental value of the stock of service-yielding consumer durable goods, and the unit's resources include net worth, current earnings and nonproperty income, and the discounted value of all expected future income.

This definition of optimal consumption should be extended further to include the value of present and expected public services, leisure time, and nonmarket goods and services. Similarly, the definition of available resources should be extended to include time available to be allocated between work and leisure, public services, and the present value of expected tax liability. Expansion of the resource constraint in this way would move the Ando–Modigliani concept toward a concept of "full income" (see Becker 1965). In addition, the Ando–Modigliani measure should be refined to adjust for differences in the size and composition of the consumption unit. Thus, the total optimal consumption figure for a household should be divided by the number of "equivalent consumer units" in the household.[3] The concept of *potential real consumption per equivalent consumer unit* is a comprehensive, theoretically based definition of economic welfare or economic position.[4]

Held up to this ideal, annual family money income has enormous shortcomings. It does not include nonmoney sources of income (in-kind transfers, capital gains, and the services of the public sector and other nonmarket activities) and it fails to exclude liability for taxes. It does not account for differences in family size and composition, nor does it reflect the value of leisure in any way. Perhaps most important, particularly in the case of the aged, the current income measure contains no information on the net value of assets held by a consuming unit.[5]

In recent years, numerous efforts, in addition to those of Duesen-

[3] See Seneca and Taussig (1971) and Nicholson (1976) for a summary of work on the measurement and use of equivalence scales in estimating economic status.

[4] Taussig (1973) and Pechman and Okner (1975) employ a similar concept.

[5] See Schultz (1965) and Taussig (1973) for a detailed discussion of many of these shortcomings.

berry, Friedman, and Ando–Modigliani have been made to extend the household money income measure toward the concept of potential real consumption or "full income." In most cases, these efforts have involved adjusting the standard household money income measure by adding or subtracting elements that account for its deviation from the "ideal" concept. By and large, such adjustments to the current money income measure have been undertaken to determine the nature and extent of the bias that using the standard indicator gives to measures of relative well-being.

One of the earliest of these efforts was undertaken by James Morgan and his associates in 1962. In their study of income and welfare in the United States, refinements were made in the definitions of both income and the consumer unit. The measurement of family well-being took account of the structure of the consuming unit (by separating complex families into "adult units"), nonmoney income (by including home production), and taxes related to income. Moreover, through use of the welfare ratio concept,[6] the needs of families of various sizes and structures were taken into account. A few years later, Morgan and his associates extended this approach through improvements in the measurement of the value of nonmarket productive activities and the adjustment for family size and needs (Morgan, Sirageldin, and Baerwaldt 1965; Sirageldin 1969), and through the inclusion of the value of leisure in the measure of economic well-being (Morgan 1968; Morgan and Smith 1969; Smith and Morgan 1970).

Also in the late 1960s, Weisbrod and Hansen (1968) further closed the gap between money income and the ideal measure by combining current income and current net worth in a single indicator of economic status (see also Projector and Weiss 1969). They accomplished this by aggregating the annual lifetime annuity value of a consuming unit's current net worth and its current annual income net of current period property income.

Subsequent efforts have focused on the definition and measurement of the recipient value of in-kind transfers and its incorporation into estimates of economic status (see Schmundt, Smolensky, and Stiefel 1975). Recognizing the inadequacy of previous approaches that valued in-kind transfers at either the cost incurred on behalf of recipients or the market value of private benefits, this approach

---

[6] This concept was first introduced into the literature by Martin H. David (1959).

values such transfers in "equivalent cash transfer units," based on the consumer unit's utility function, disposable cash income, and the combination of in-kind programs for which the family is eligible.

Whereas each of these empirical efforts has addressed the shortfall of current income from the "ideal" measure of economic status on a piecemeal basis, a number of recent studies have attempted simultaneously to incorporate several of the proposed adjustments into a measure of economic welfare. These include studies of the age-specific inequality of economic welfare (Taussig 1973), the effect of public cash and in-kind programs on the distribution of economic welfare among the aged (Moon 1977), and the target efficiency of government programs indexed by a more comprehensive measure of economic welfare than current money income (Smeeding 1975).

The Present Study

This monograph is organized as follows. Chapter 2 presents the procedures followed in estimating earnings capacity for various family units, describes the data sources used in the study, and discusses the weaknesses of our measure of earnings capacity. Chapter 3 is concerned with the degree to which earnings capacity is utilized by the population as a whole and, in particular, by various groups identified by age, race, sex, and economic status. This chapter also analyzes the relative contributions to observed income inequality of both variations in earnings capacity and variations in capacity utilization. Chapters 4 and 5 focus on the lower tail of the distribution of economic status—the families living in poverty. In Chapter 4, the earnings capacity concept is used as the basis for defining poverty. The demographic composition of those who are poor as measured by earnings capacity (the earnings capacity poor) is described and compared to that of those who are poor as measured by current income (the current income poor). The concept of the target efficiency of public programs is introduced in Chapter 5 and employed in estimating the extent to which various public transfer programs concentrate their benefits on the earnings capacity poor as compared to the current income poor. Finally, the problem of racial differences in income and earnings capacity is analyzed in Chapter 6. The contribution of labor market discrimination to observed black-white earnings differences is estimated by using the earnings capacity concept. Chapter 7 summarizes the main findings of the study, draws the important policy implications from these findings, and presents some suggestions for further research both to improve the estimation of earnings capacity and to apply the concept to additional policy problems.

2
The Measurement of
Earnings Capacity

We have discussed the conceptual weaknesses of using annual money income as a measure of economic status, and we have introduced an alternative to measures based on income. This alternative measure, called earnings capacity, is defined as the income stream that would be generated if a household unit employed its human and physical assets to capacity. We turn now to our procedures for deriving estimates of earnings capacity for individuals and households.

Data and Methodology

In estimating earnings capacity for individual families, we use two different microdata sources. The first is the 1971 Current Population Survey (CPS), with individual observations aged to be representative of the United States population and its demographic and economic characteristics in 1973. The survey observations are also modified to yield a national unemployment rate of 4.9%.[1] The second data file is the Panel Study of Income Dynamics conducted by the Institute for Social Research of the University of Michigan (see Morgan *et al.* 1974). While the CPS contains far more individual observations than does the Panel Study—50,000 families compared with 5000 families—the Panel Study is a much richer data source, containing data on family characteristics, income sources, and assets. For most of the analysis, sample size is judged to outweigh the availability of data on additional family characteristics. Consequently, most of the analysis focuses on the results from the CPS data source. In some cases, however, the availability of additional variables leads to reliance on the Panel Study data. The discussion indicates which data source is being used at a particular time and points out differences in results between data sources.

In order to derive an indicator of a household's relative economic status that is largely independent of the unit's tastes for income and temporary fluctuations in its income, we construct the following measure of gross earnings capacity for a family (EC_F):

$$EC_F = EC_H + EC_S, \tag{2.1}$$

where

EC_H = head's imputed annual earnings capacity at 50–52 weeks of full-time work;

EC_S = spouse's imputed annual earnings capacity at 50–52 weeks of full-time work.

The earnings capacities of the head and spouse are imputed on the basis of their demographic characteristics from four regression equations in which annual earned income is the dependent variable. The

---

[1] The March 1971 CPS is aged to allow for demographic changes, economic growth, and inflation through 1973. In addition, the 6% unemployment rate of 1970 is adjusted to 4.9% by randomly assigning unemployment and duration of unemployment to groups identified by age, sex, occupation, and unemployment experience using the RIM model developed by the Urban Institute. For a more detailed discussion of the adjustment of the 1971 data, see McClung, Moeller, and Siguel (1971). We use this data base because of its combination of extensive background characteristics of head and spouse and large number of observations. The latter characteristic is essential for developing reliable estimates of earnings capacity for narrowly defined socioeconomic groups.

independent variables are chosen to conform to conventional human capital models. They include age, years of schooling, race, marital status, and location.[2] In addition, dummy variables for weeks worked and part- or full-time work during the employed weeks are included. Only individuals with positive earnings are included in the sample from which the earnings equations are estimated. Separate regression equations are estimated for white and black men and for white and black women. Through these regressions, average full-time earnings of men and women with different sets of human capital and demographic characteristics are estimated. As equation (2.1) indicates, earnings capacities of older children or other adults in a family unit are not included in the definition of gross earnings capacity.[3]

Reliance on the human capital framework leads to a number of a priori expectations regarding the size and direction of the relationship between the independent variables and earnings. Consistent with that framework, earnings in the early and middle adult years are expected to increase with age because of job experience and on-the-job training. In the later adult years, earnings are expected to decrease as skills become obsolete and physical and mental capacities deteriorate. Earnings are also expected to increase with education and training, as measured by years of schooling. Previous

[2] These variables are consistent with those conventionally employed in empirical analyses of wage or earnings differences based on the human capital approach. While an effort is made to include only exogenous or permanent individual characteristics as explanatory variables, some of the independent variables clearly contain an element of choice. For example, while earnings depend positively upon the productivity associated with education, the amount of education an individual ultimately attains may also depend upon his expected earnings. Similar elements of choice affect the marital status and location variables. An ideal procedure would be to specify a complete structural model containing a series of equations in which each dependent variable is a function of factors that are clearly exogenous to it. Such a model could then be estimated as a series of simultaneous equations. The limitations of the data used in this study make this procedure impossible; in effect, the approach chosen yields structural estimates that represent the conditional expectation of annual earned income given the individual's human capital and demographic characteristics, that are assumed to be fixed in the short run. For a more complete discussion of the specification of wage and earnings models based on human capital theory, see Blinder (1974) and Mincer (1974).

[3] In one of our two data sources, data on years of schooling are unavailable for household members other than the head and spouse. The omission of the earnings capacity of other adults can affect comparisons of the earnings capacity and current income measures of economic status, particularly with respect to family size rankings. See Chapter 4, note 6.

studies have shown that the effect of several of these variables on earnings varies with age. Hence, the regression equations are specified to permit such interactions between these variables and age.

The use of separate equations for race and sex groups presumes the existence of labor market discrimination and allows other possible differences in structural relationships. For individuals with otherwise identical characteristics, earnings are expected to be smaller for blacks than for whites, and for women than for men. Similarly, differences in earnings reflect both regional differences in cost of living and labor demand and real differences in productivity not captured by our other variables. Because earnings are expected to be positively related to experience and on-the-job training, it is anticipated that women in categories with smaller probabilities of recent work experience (for example, married women with children) will have lower earnings than those in categories with greater probabilities of recent work experience (for example, single women without children).

Although experimentation is undertaken with both a linear and a log-linear model, only the estimates derived from the log-linear model are reported, for several reasons. First, contrasts between economic status as measured by current income and by earnings capacity are quite insensitive to the functional form used in the development of the estimates of earnings capacity. Second, for a number of a priori reasons, the log-linear model is preferable, the most important consideration being the required nonnegativity of predicted earnings from a log-linear model. In addition, it is likely that the variance in earnings is smaller with smaller amounts of human capital. The log-linear model neither requires nonnegative predicted values nor relates the variance in earned income positively to the level of human capital. Finally, the log-linear model yields a somewhat better fit.

The estimated earnings functions are presented in Table 2.1. The coefficients on the variables are as expected. Earnings of both men and women first increase and then decrease with age. Similarly, earned income is positively related to years of schooling. Consistent with previous studies, the effect of education on earnings increases with age—but the coefficient is statistically significant only for white men. Comparing the coefficients for age and years of schooling for blacks to those for whites indicates that the education–earnings and

Table 2.1

EARNINGS FUNCTIONS FOR BLACK AND WHITE MEN AND WOMEN

Independent variable	Men		Women	
	White coefficient	Black coefficient	White coefficient	Black coefficient
Years of schooling	.0212 (3.0)	−.0088 (−.4)	−.0106 (−.7)	−.0229 (−.7)
Years of schooling^2	.0007 (3.2)	.0017 (2.8)	.0033 (6.5)	.0047 (4.3)
Age	.0711 (33.3)	.0525 (7.1)	.0479 (13.3)	.0234 (2.2)
Age^2	−.0008 (−42.6)	−.0007 (−10.0)	−.0006 (−18.1)	−.0004 (−4.0)
Age × years of schooling	.0005 (5.6)	.0004 (1.5)	.0001 (.5)	.0004 (.8)
Weeks worked				
1–13	−1.9636 (−85.8)	−2.0173 (−31.1)	−2.2937 (−111.8)	−2.0924 (−39.4)
14–26	−.8201 (−44.2)	−.8324 (−17.1)	−.9790 (−48.0)	−.8835 (−16.4)
27–39	−.4103 (−27.2)	−.3742 (−8.5)	−.4851 (−22.6)	−.4215 (−7.8)
40–47	−.2067 (−13.9)	−.2563 (−5.9)	−.2395 (−9.8)	−.2097 (−3.4)
48–49	−.1434 (−7.1)	−.0970 (−1.6)	−.1446 (−4.0)	−.0124 (−.1)
50–52	—	—	—	—

Full- or part-time work during week				
Full-time	—	—	—	—
Part-time	−.9105 (−51.0)	−.9827 (−21.2)	−.9162 (−61.3)	−.8767 (−22.4)
Location				
Northeast	−.0149 (−1.6)	−.0197 (−.5)	.1292 (7.5)	.1154 (2.2)
North Central	—	—	—	—
South	−.1120 (−12.2)	−.2362 (−7.5)	−.0416 (−2.5)	−.2017 (−4.4)
West	−.0541 (−5.3)	.0132 (.3)	−.0299 (1.6)	−.0316 (−.5)
SMSA suburb	.1542 (18.7)	.2664 (7.1)	.1790 (11.7)	.2647 (4.9)
SMSA central city	.0685 (8.0)	.1609 (5.7)	.1883 (12.2)	.2133 (5.2)
Nonurban	—	—	—	—
Marital status				
Not married, no children			.1243 (6.1)	−.0113 (−.2)
Not married, with children			.0524 (2.1)	−.0378 (−.9)
Married, no children			.1261 (7.8)	−.0030 (−.1)
Constant	7.2901 (96.8)	7.6699 (32.5)	7.1515 (49.0)	7.5754 (20.3)
r^2	.5252	.6068	.6026	.6337
F	1813.7819	266.8581	1498.4130	247.2347

NOTE: t values appear in parentheses.

age–earnings profiles of blacks are considerably flatter than those of whites. Location has a significant effect on the earnings of both men and women. It is not surprising that both men and women—particularly blacks—residing in the South earn less than men and women in other parts of the country. The differences range from 4% less than those living in the North Central region for white women to 24% less for black men. The difference between living in a small town or rural area and in an urban area is even more pronounced in three of the four cases. Married men earn significantly more than single men, and single women without children earn more than married women without children. The latter, in turn, earn more than single women with children, and married women with children earn the least of the four groups. Finally, the effect of work status on the earnings of black and white men and women is profound. The R^2 in the regressions ranges from .52 for white men to .63 for black women.

Using these estimated coefficients, an individual's demographic characteristics, and the assumption that capacity work effort entails full-time employment for 50–52 weeks per year, we assign every family head and spouse in the sample an earnings capacity, EC_H or EC_S.[4] For each individual, then, the values of the two employment variables in the regression equation are fixed at full time and 50–52 weeks and the values of the remaining variables in the equation are the individual's observed human capital and demographic characteristics. Each individual's imputed earnings capacity is obtained by choosing the regression equation corresponding to the individual's race and sex, multiplying the value of each of the remaining variables by the coefficient associated with it in that regression equation, and aggregating these products over the variables. As a result, any two individuals with the same human capital and demographic characteristics (race, sex, education, and so forth) are assigned the same earnings capacity.

For some of the analyses, a further adjustment to these estimates of capacity is made before they are aggregated into an estimate of household earnings capacity. This procedure just leads to estimates of individual capacity in which all individuals of the same age, sex, race, years of schooling, location, and work status are assigned an

---

[4] This specification presumes that deviation from full-time, full-year work is attributable to choice. As described later, it is this choice that is suppressed in the estimation of earnings capacity.

earnings capacity equal to the mean of the cell within which they are included. All variance within cells is thus artificially eliminated. To the extent that such variance within cells is attributable to unobserved human capital differences or to chance, its suppression is inappropriate for many purposes. Assigning the cell mean tends to exaggerate the effect on earnings of the independent variables included in the regression, to understate the inequality in the distribution of earnings capacity, and to overstate the probability that individuals with a set of characteristics associated with poverty will be poor.

To avoid this artificial compression of the earnings capacity distribution, we distribute individual observations within a cell randomly about the cell mean. This distribution is accomplished through a random number generator technique that incorporates the assumption that the distribution of observations within cells is normal, with a standard deviation equal to the standard deviation of the regression equation.[5] From this procedure, the mean value of each cell is retained, but a normal distribution of observations within cells is achieved. The randomized values for head and spouse are designated as $\widehat{EC}_H$ and $\widehat{EC}_S$. Summing these randomized estimates within a household yields an alternative measure of gross earnings capacity, $\widetilde{EC}_F$:

$$\widetilde{EC}_F = \widetilde{EC}_H + \widetilde{EC}_S. \tag{2.2}$$

However, neither EC_F nor $\widetilde{EC}_F$ fully reflects a family's economic position. Neither measure includes an estimate of the capacity return to the physical assets—such as stocks, bonds, and real estate—possessed by a household. Moreover, both measures implicitly assume that everyone can work 50–52 weeks per year, while in fact health limitations and unemployment may prevent some individuals from achieving this capacity level. Finally, neither EC_F nor $\widetilde{EC}_F$ take account of the costs of working. In order to account for these factors, we modify the basic definitions of earnings capacity in a number of ways.

[5] The random number generator routine *RANNB* generates a sequence of pseudo-random numbers with a normal (Gaussian) distribution with mean 0 and variance 1 by the method of Box and Muller (1958). See Academic Computing Center (1969) for a description of computation procedures.

To take account of returns to assets and intrafamily transfers, we define the following more comprehensive earnings capacity variables:

$$GEC = EC_F + Y \qquad\qquad (2.3)$$

$$G\widetilde{E}C = \widetilde{E}C_F + Y, \qquad\qquad (2.4)$$

where

$Y =$ income from interest, dividends, rents, alimony, and miscellaneous other sources (not including government transfers).

Because income from interest, dividends, and rents is a measure (albeit a crude one)[6] of a household's ability to generate income from its assets, such income should be counted in ascertaining the household's economic status. In adding these actual income flows to human capital earnings capacity, we implicitly assume that a family's assets other than human capital are being used at capacity. Most transfer payments, on the other hand, are excluded from our measure of economic status, because income from transfer payments does not result from a family's ability to generate income.[7]

Some individuals do not work full time, full year because of either health disabilities or insufficient aggregate demand. To take account

---

[6] Some assets, such as home equity, have no reported monetary return. Hence, *GEC* and *G$\widehat{E}$C* underestimate the earnings capacity of families receiving services from owner-occupied housing (see Weisbrod and Hansen 1968).

[7] In earlier work on earnings capacity, we mistakenly asserted that Social Security payments and government and private pensions are included in our measures of earnings capacity (see Garfinkel and Haveman 1974; 1977). There are at least two good reasons for including these transfers. First, Social Security payments and pensions can be viewed as substitutes for savings. Second, they can be viewed as flows of income from assets. On the other hand, because such (largely) public transfer programs have as part of their rationale the provision of an income flow to enable the substitution of leisure for work, it does not seem reasonable to add such transfers to an estimate of income flows that assumes no consumption of leisure. Moreover, including these transfers in our measures of earnings capacity would only increase the contrasts between earnings capacity and current income that we identify in the text. For example, we show that if poverty is defined in terms of earnings capacity rather than current income, a greater proportion of the poor live in families with workers and with nonaged heads. Including Social Security payments and pensions in our measure of earnings capacity would have increased the measured incomes of families with aged heads without jobs, thereby increasing further our estimate of the proportion of poor who live in households headed by nonaged workers.

of such exogenous limitations on economic capacity, the earnings capacity estimates of the head and spouse are adjusted by multiplying them by an adjustment factor when such characteristics are present. This factor is defined as $\gamma = (50 - W_{su})/50$, where W_{su} is reported weeks not worked because of sickness, disability, or unemployment. After this adjustment, the following earnings capacity measures are obtained:

$$GEC^* = EC_H \cdot \gamma + EC_S \cdot \gamma + Y \qquad (2.5)$$

$$G\widetilde{E}C^* = \widetilde{EC}_H \cdot \gamma + \widetilde{EC}_S \cdot \gamma + Y. \qquad (2.6)$$

Adjusting for illness and unemployment builds some temporary reductions in income into the earnings capacity measure for an individual family. Nevertheless, there are several strong arguments for such adjustments. Although many reported disabilities are permanent, some reflect temporary illness. Limitations in our data make it impossible to separate reductions in employment caused by permanent disabilities from those caused by temporary disabilities. Moreover, while all unemployment and impermanent illness cause temporary reductions in an individual's earnings capacity, both are permanent phenomena from the perspective of the overall economy. Most important, we assume that, for the most part, neither differences in unemployment nor differences in health status reflect taste differences, the differences our measure of economic status is designed to eliminate.

GEC^* and $G\widetilde{E}C^*$, then, measure family economic status as a flow of potential gross income and reflect explicit judgments regarding the definitions of capacity work effort and capacity use of physical assets. They make no allowance for the fact that the real costs entailed by attainment of this capacity may vary among families. Some of these costs are associated with the type of work undertaken and are therefore reflected in the wage rate. Others result from obstacles to employment caused by circumstances of family structure or location, in combination with socially established standards for overcoming these obstacles. Young children, for example, make it hard for both parents to work. Parents can overcome this difficulty by arranging care for their children that meets acceptable standards. From the perspective of the individual family, economic status depends on the magnitude of the latter type of costs, and an alternative measure of family economic status should therefore consider them explicitly.

Clearly the largest component of these costs, and the component that varies most among families, is the need to provide care for children. The contribution of children to family economic status is a complex matter. In most cases, the presence of children conveys utility to the parents; an ideal measure of economic welfare would reflect this value. In an ideal framework, the net benefit of children would equal the gross flow of satisfaction they convey less the costs required for their care. If it is assumed that the presence of children conveys no utility, only the subtraction of the cost of child care is necessary. Even though our gross measures of economic status, GEC^* and $\widetilde{GEC}^*$, do not reflect the value of children, we do adjust these values for each family by subtracting an estimate of the minimum cost of an acceptable level of child care. The justification for this procedure rests on the following considerations: First, not all children are wanted, particularly in families at the lower end of the income distribution. Moreover, if economic welfare is viewed from the perspective of the children, our procedure of simulating the returns from market work of mothers implies a loss that is not accounted for in the GEC measures. Finally, the adjustment does reflect the costs of overcoming the obstacle to attaining full earnings capacity created by children in the home. Consequently, in addition to the GEC measures, we calculate a measure of net earnings capacity, (NEC^*) for each family, defined as follows:[8]

$$NEC^* = GEC^* - (\$1510 \cdot \text{number of children aged 5 or younger})$$
$$+ (\$376 \cdot \text{number of children aged 6–14}). \qquad (2.7)$$

Weaknesses in the Measure of Earnings Capacity

For numerous reasons, our measures of earnings capacity deviate from the concept of earnings capacity. In the adjustments for

---

[8] Data on costs of child care are derived from 1968 estimates adjusted for inflation. The 1968 estimates of the minimum dollar amount required to achieve "acceptable" child care are from B. Bernstein and P. Giacchino, "Costs of Day Care, Implications for Public Policy," *City Almanac,* August 1971, as reported by Krashinsky (1975).

unemployment and illness, for example, three shortcomings should be noted. First, to the extent that differences in unemployment and health status are either related to taste or temporary, our adjustment results in an underestimate of the part of the difference between earnings capacity and current income that is attributable to taste or to temporary changes in income. Second, at least some of the time an individual spends unemployed is attributable not to the absence of a job but to the absence of a job that the individual deems suitable. For this reason, the adjusted earnings capacity measure understates earnings capacity for some individuals. Third, there are individuals whose estimated earnings capacity is not subject to this adjustment: some who have been unemployed for long periods and dropped out of the labor force and others who are neither seeking nor holding employment because of illness or disability. The earnings capacity of these individuals is overstated relative to that of individuals with identical characteristics who are in the labor force. It follows that our estimates of earnings capacity for groups with relatively low rates of labor force participation are biased upwards compared to those for groups with higher rates of participation.[9]

Another weakness of our estimates of earnings capacity is the relatively crude estimation of the capacity return from physical assets and of the costs of achieving capacity work effort. For the latter, only the costs of child care are deducted. Moreover, it could be argued that our adjustment for the costs of child care is too high for families who can rely on relatives, older children, or friends for child care and that observed expenses for child care vary positively with *GEC*. With respect to the first point, it is reasonable to expect that the real costs to a family of securing child care by exploiting relatives or friends exceed out-of-pocket expenses. Consequently, the dollar values we employ may not be as far from real values as they first appear. On the second point, it should be noted that our estimates are designed

[9] This bias is small, however, given that the ratio of adjusted to unadjusted aggregate earnings capacity for the population (not including the aged, students, or the military) is .97. Adjustments for nonparticipants in the labor force could have been imputed from adjustments for participants with similar characteristics. This approach was not followed, however, for two reasons. First, the absence of a close relationship between demographic characteristics of labor force participants and illness, disability, and unemployment would have caused the adjustment for nonparticipants to be little more than random assignment. Second, and more important, expected illness, disability, and unemployment themselves affect the choice of whether or not to participate in the labor force.

to reflect the costs of meeting socially imposed standards for over-coming this obstacle to work effort, rather than actual family choices; hence the use of minimum costs required to obtain a level of care that is officially designated as "acceptable."[10]

The most important shortcoming of our measures of earnings capacity derives from the fact that our regressions fail to capture all of the determinants of earned income. Recall that our regressions explain only 50% to 60% of the variance in earnings. Moreover, a large portion of the variance for which we are able to account comes from variation in hours and weeks worked. In judging whether our measure of earnings capacity or actual earnings is a better indicator of a family's real economic welfare, the critical issue is the relative importance of taste and transitory phenomena versus unmeasured determinants of earnings capacity in explaining observed earnings.

To compare our *measure* of earnings capacity with the measure of economic status based on current income, consider two individuals of identical age, sex, race, years of schooling, and location who have actual earnings of $10,000 and $5000. The mean earnings capacity for their cell is $7500, and our procedure assigns each of them an earnings capacity of $7500. We hold that the two individuals have the same earnings capacity—the same potential level of economic welfare—and that the gap in actual income is caused by differences in taste or transitory effects on their earnings. Our procedure is incorrect if the gap is actually attributable to the systematic and persistent effects of unobserved variables.

It is possible that the $5000 difference between the earnings of the two individuals in this example is attributable entirely to differences in physical or mental ability: One individual may be handsome, the other plain; one strong, the other weak; one bright, the other dull. Our data do not capture these differences. Similarly, the differences may be attributable to differences in the quality of their education or to differences in the demand for their labor services.[11] Finally, the difference may be caused by chance. Luck experienced early in a

[10] We again emphasize that our purpose is to develop a measure of relative economic position among households, not a measure of utility. For the latter purpose, considering children only as obstacles to work effort would not be appropriate.

[11] It should be noted that our estimated earnings functions reflect a human capital approach to explaining earnings differences. Those who adhere to a supply and demand framework in explaining the distribution of earnings might judge that we have neglected the demand (or opportunities) side of the market (see Tinbergen 1975).

career may persist. Clearly, a part of the difference in earnings between individuals with identical measured characteristics, which we attribute to differences in taste and transitory effects, can be attributed to the effects of unmeasured variables. Whether actual earnings or our measure of earnings capacity is a superior indicator of real economic welfare depends upon the relative magnitude of taste and transitory effects in comparison with unmeasured differences in earnings capacity in explaining the differences in actual earnings among individuals with identical measured characteristics. Throughout the monograph, we take care to call attention to cases where we believe the effects of unmeasured differences may be significant. Still, because authors are likely to take excessive pride in their own creations, the reader should constantly bear in mind the potential biases that arise because of unmeasured differences in earnings capacity and, more generally, the distinction between the concept of earnings capacity and our particular estimates of it.

3

Economic Inequality and the Utilization of Earnings Capacity

This chapter is the first of three in which the concept and empirical measurement of earnings capacity are employed in analyzing characteristics of economic status among various socioeconomic groups. In this chapter, earnings capacity—as a measure of the ability of individuals and families to generate income in the markets for labor and capital—is set off against the actual earnings of individuals and families. This allows us to gauge the extent to which individuals and families utilize their earnings capacity in much the same way as we gauge the utilization of capacity by individual industries or by the economy as a whole. Next, differences among various groups in the population in the utilization of earnings capacity are examined. Finally, the degree of inequality in the distribution of earnings capacity is compared with the degree of inequality in the distribution of actual earnings and income. The objective here is to discern the relative contributions to observed earnings inequality of both earnings capacity and its utilization. This analysis is followed in Chapters 4 and 5 by an examination of the composition of those at the bottom of the distribution—the earnings capacity poor—and an evaluation of the effectiveness of various income transfer proposals in targeting their benefits on this same group.

Although comparison of capacity utilization patterns among various population groups is of intrinsic interest, additional considerations motivate this analysis. First, pervading the national debate on social policy has been the issue of the "worthiness" of the beneficiaries of public programs. Thus, extension of assistance to poor families has been opposed by some on the grounds that at least some poor persons are in that state because they do not use their capacities as effectively as those who are not poor. Similarly, the high incidence of poverty among blacks has been regarded by some as evidence of a lack of motivation or a failure to take advantage of earnings opportunities.[1] With a measure of earnings capacity, the basis for these assertions can be examined.

A second reason for analyzing patterns of capacity utilization is to discern the relationship between differential utilization rates and observed income inequality. While the substantial and persistent observed income inequality in the United States stems from numerous interdependent factors, these factors can be partitioned into two categories—inequality of earnings capacity and variation in the utilization of earnings capacity. Through analysis of both factors, the relative contribution of each to observed inequality can be determined.[2]

Before proceeding, we should again emphasize that the measurement of earnings capacity is, of necessity, not free of arbitrary assumptions. There exist a wide variety of earnings capacity concepts: Each has a particular meaning and each might be appropriate for answering particular questions. For example, in all of the earnings capacity estimates used here, a 2000-hour work year is taken to be capacity. Implicit in this assumption is the proposition that the 40-hour work week and the 50-week work year set a full employment norm. Different assumptions would have yielded alternative estimates of earnings capacity. Additional assumptions are necessary in adjusting for unemployment and disability and estimating net earn-

[1] These assertions can be tested only partially by the earnings capacity concept. If a particular group lacks motivation and manifests this lack by seeking or accepting jobs with lower rates of pay (presumably, less demanding jobs), our analysis will not discover it. Indeed, if the labor market discrimination against such groups exists, its effect on wage rates, in all likelihood, cannot be distinguished statistically from the effect of lack of motivation. See Chapter 6 for additional analysis of this problem.

[2] See Jencks *et al.* (1972) and Thurow (1975) for other efforts to partition the sources of income inequality.

ings capacity from gross earnings capacity by deducting the costs of child care. While assumptions of this sort affect the absolute level of estimated earnings capacity for any particular individual or family, they are not likely to bias seriously estimates of earnings capacity for the groups of individuals or families discussed here. Although one could quarrel with the levels of our estimates of capacity for individual household units, we judge that this criticism is not likely to extend to our analysis of patterns of aggregate utilization of earnings capacity and the utilization of capacity by various population groups.

Aggregate Capacity Utilization and Its Components

In this section, estimates of the utilization of earnings capacity are presented at the macroeconomic level. In addition to estimating the aggregate differential between actual earnings and earnings capacity, we attempt to identify some of the more important components of this differential. This attempt is analogous to efforts to measure and account for the differential between actual Gross National Product (GNP) and potential (or full-employment) GNP—the emphasis is on the performance of the economy as a whole.

In Table 3.1 are presented estimates, for subgroups of the population, of aggregate earnings capacity, aggregate earnings, aggregate earnings capacity gap (aggregate earnings capacity less aggregate earnings), aggregate capacity utilization rate (CUR), and percentage contributed to the total earnings capacity gap.

While total earnings capacity for the economy is estimated to be $1132 billion, actual earnings in 1973 are only $670 billion, or 59% of the total. This gap between capacity and earnings is accounted for by several factors, only one of which might be interpreted as implying that the work force is heavily opting for leisure rather than work. A substantial share of the differential is accounted for by individuals over 65 who have chosen (or been forced) either to retire or to substitute part-time or part-year work for full-time work. As the second row in the table shows, $89 billion, or 19% of the total gap, is accounted for by the aged population, which has a measured rate of capacity utilization of 29%. Although a substantial proportion of the aged undoubtedly work less than full time voluntarily, we over-

Table 3.1

THE AGGREGATE EARNINGS CAPACITY GAP AND ITS COMPONENTS (BILLIONS OF DOLLARS)

	Gross earnings capacity	Actual earnings	Capacity gap	Capacity utilization rate	Percentage of total capacity gap
1. Total population	1132	670	462	59	100
2. Aged population	125	36	89	29	19
3. Nonaged population	1007	634	373	63	81
4. Nonaged, nonstudent, non-military population	992	630	362	64	78
5. Nonaged, nonstudent, non-military population adjusted for health and unemployment	964	630	334	65	72 (100)
a. Male heads	547	478	69	87	15 (21)
b. Wives	313	87	226	27	49 (68)
c. Female heads	81	42	39	52	8 (11)
6. Nonaged, nonstudent, non-military population adjusted for health, unemployment, and child care	964	687	277	71	60

NOTE: For groups 1 through 4, the earnings capacity estimate is GEC, the gross measure unadjusted for unemployment or health, and the estimate of earnings is GE, the sum of the actual earnings of the head and spouse plus unearned income (Y). For group 5, the earnings capacity estimate is GEC^*, the GEC measure adjusted for the constraints imposed by illness, disability, and unemployment. For the three groups of individuals—5a, b, and c—the earnings capacity for individual x is defined as $EC_x[(50 - W_{su})/50] = EC^*$. The disparity in definitions between 5 and its components—a, b, and c—is caused by the inclusion of unearned income (Y) in the estimate for the aggregate. Although the measures of both capacity and earnings are affected by the inclusion or exclusion of Y, the differential between capacity and earnings is not.

estimate the earnings capacity of the aged because of our inability to adjust the estimates for health and institutional limitations on work adequately.

The balance of Table 3.1 focuses on the nonaged population. As row 3 indicates, the difference between capacity and actual earnings for the nonaged population is $373 billion, implying that this group has an earnings capacity utilization rate (CUR) of 63%. More than 80% of the total gap between capacity and actual earnings is accounted for by this group.

Row 4 contains estimates for the nonaged population, also excluding students and members of the armed forces; but this accounts for very little of the total gap between capacity and earnings and reduces the total earnings capacity gap of the population under consideration by only $11 billion, from $373 billion to $362 billion. The estimates in the first four rows of the table are not adjusted for constraints on earnings capacity caused by illness, disability, or unemployment. In row 5, estimates for the same population as that shown in row 4 are presented after adjustments for these constraints. These adjustments reduce the estimate of earnings capacity by $28 billion and shrink the estimate of the difference between earnings capacity and actual earnings from $362 billion to $334 billion, implying a CUR of 65%.[3]

This earnings capacity gap of $334 billion can be allocated among the three primary types of adults that compose the nonaged population—male family heads, wives, and female family heads. As Table 3.1 (rows 5a, 5b, and 5c) indicates, male heads have a much higher CUR (87%) than do either female heads (52%) or wives (27%). Only 15% of the total earnings capacity gap is attributable to nonaged men who are neither students nor members of the armed forces and who are not limited in the amount of work they can do by either health problems or unemployment. Nearly 50% of the total gap is contributed by wives and another 8% by female heads.

The low CUR of wives (27%) and, to a lesser extent, female heads (52%) should not be taken as indicators of the extent to which these groups engage in productive activity. In large measure, they have low relative earnings because their child care and homemaking activities do not pass through a market and are not rewarded with earned

---

[3] Of the total adjustment of $28 billion, $18 billion is accounted for by men; $18 billion is accounted for by involuntary unemployment; about $10 billion is accounted for by illness or disability.

income. The fact that such productive activities do not pass through a market contributes to the weakness of this or any other concept of aggregate economic capacity and capacity utilization. In order to strengthen our concept, we impute a market value to these activities, a step that substantially reduces the estimated differential between the earnings and the earnings capacity of women.

The earnings estimates shown in row 6 of the table include an estimate of the market value of the child care provided by wives and female family heads with children. For wives and female heads who do not work outside the home at all, the market value of the child care services they provide is estimated to be equal to the estimates of the cost of child care described in Chapter 2. For women who work part time and/or part year, the estimate of the value of the services they provide is reduced in proportion to the amount of time they work.[4] This imputation raises earnings of wives and female heads by $57 billion, thereby reducing the earnings capacity gap to $277 billion. Consequently, the CUR for the nonaged population increases to 71%. It should be noted, however, that we make only a crude imputation for the value of child care; no attempt is made to include the value of other nonmarket work in the home. Thus, the earnings estimate in line 6 remains an underestimate of the total value of market and nonmarket activities, and, consequently, 71% remains an underestimate of CUR.

Patterns of Capacity Utilization within the Nonaged Population

Within these overall dimensions of aggregate earnings capacity and its utilization, there is likely to be substantial variation in capacity utilization among subgroups of the population. Because an individual's rate of capacity utilization (CUR) is positively related to his or her work effort (or labor supply), factors that account for variation in individual labor supply also explain the variation in individual capacity utilization rates. These factors include (a) income; (b) the

[4] We assume that part-time work is equivalent to 20 hours per week. Thus, for a woman who works 40 part-time weeks, the estimated cost of child care is equal to $(800/2000) \cdot$ (imputed total child care costs).

rewards for and costs of working; (c) tastes for income versus leisure, and (d) the availability of work.[5] For example, because of child care costs, a woman with children will tend to have a lower CUR than a woman without children. Similarly, men will tend to have a higher CUR than women because of differences in the taste for market work rather than nonmarket work that result from different social expectations for men and women. In addition, because income transfer programs simultaneously increase the incomes of beneficiaries and reduce the rewards to them from working, individuals eligible for such programs—for example, female heads of households—will tend to work less, ceteris paribus, than ineligible individuals. In contrast to these predictions, expectations regarding the relationship of CUR to the level of earnings capacity are not so clear cut. On the one hand, individuals with high capacity will tend to work less because they have more income; on the other hand, they will tend to work more because their reward for working is higher.

Throughout this section, the CUR is defined as the ratio of actual earnings to earnings capacity, where earnings capacity is adjusted for limitations on work resulting from illness, disability, and unemployment but does not include a family's nonemployment income.[6] In addition, the nonrandomized estimates of earnings capacity are used.[7] That is, for individuals,

$$CUR_x = \text{Actual Earnings}_x / EC_x^*, \tag{3.1}$$

[5] See Watts and Cain (1971) and Garfinkel and Masters (1978) for analyses of these factors in the context of labor supply.

[6] Inclusion of nonemployment income would artificially bias the capacity utilization rate towards one, since it would appear in both the numerator and the denominator of the ratio. Other things being equal, therefore, those with higher proportions of nonemployment income would have higher capacity utilization rates.

[7] Use of the randomized estimates would create an artificial negative relationship between earnings capacity and the capacity utilization rate and hence distort our analysis of this relationship. As described in Chapter 2, the randomized estimates are obtained by applying a random shock variable to full-time, full-year earnings imputations based on fitted earnings functions. Within each cell with the same values for age, education, location, etc., the estimates of capacity are distributed normally around the mean estimate of earnings capacity for that cell. If everyone worked at capacity, earnings within each cell would be equal to the mean estimate of earnings capacity for that cell. Because of the random shock, some individuals are assigned higher and other individuals lower values of earnings capacity. Since the expected value of earnings for those assigned higher or lower values of capacity is still the mean, in using the randomized estimates we would have artificially constructed a negative relationship between capacity and its utilization.

and for families,

$$CUR = (E_H + E_S)\big/(EC_H{}^* + EC_S{}^*). \qquad (3.2)$$

Table 3.2 presents two sets of CUR estimates for subgroups of the nonaged population distinguished by race, sex, and marital status. In the top half of the table, the observed mean CUR is shown. Several interesting patterns should be noted. A comparison of whites with blacks indicates that the average white unit has a slightly higher CUR than the average black unit—61% compared to 58%. While this pattern holds for all men, whether married or single, the average black woman tends to have a substantially higher CUR than the average white woman—43% compared to 31%. This result is caused by the higher labor force participation rates of married black women relative to married white women. For this group, the CUR is 42% for blacks and 27% for whites.

Also, single men have a much lower observed CUR than married men in both racial groups. While some, perhaps even all, of this difference can be attributed to differences in taste and in social and financial pressure to work between these two groups, a portion of the difference may reflect an overestimation of the earnings capacity of single men relative to married men. Physical and mental disabilities not captured by our data may simultaneously reduce both true earnings capacity and the probability of marriage. Finally, it should be noted that single women utilize their capacity less than single men but more than married women and female heads of households.

These observed CUR estimates, however, may be misleading as indicators of the relationship of race, sex, or marital status to the utilization of earnings capacity. For example, if married men, on average, have higher earnings capacity than single men, and if CUR is positively associated with earnings capacity, a part of the observed CUR differential between married and single men will be due to the difference in earnings capacity rather than to marital status. This problem is particularly serious in comparisons of the rate of capacity utilization among racial groups. Because of fewer years of schooling, among other things, the mean earnings capacity of blacks is substantially lower than that of whites. If, in general, the CUR is higher for high-capacity households than for low-capacity households, blacks will be observed to have a lower rate of capacity utilization than whites, for this reason alone. Before the relationship of race

Table 3.2

OBSERVED AND ADJUSTED CAPACITY UTILIZATION RATES, BY SEX, MARITAL
STATUS, AND RACE: NONAGED POPULATION

	All	White	Black
	Observed Capacity Utilization Rates (*CUR*)		
All families and individuals	.61	.61	.58
All men	.85	.86	.80
Married men	.88	.89	.84
Single men	.66	.66	.65
All women	.32	.31	.43
Married women	.28	.27	.42
Female heads	.42	.42	.41
Single women	.55	.55	.52
	Adjusted Capacity Utilization Rates (*ACUR*)[a]		
All families and individuals	.65	.64	.70
All men	.84	.84	.84
Married men	.87	.88	.86
Single men	.68	.68	.74
All women	.33	.33	.42
Married women	.33	.33	.39
Female heads	.46	.45	.52
Single women	.64	.64	.70

[a] See Footnote 8 and text.

to capacity utilization can be estimated, this earnings capacity effect
must be eliminated.

This confounding of effects can be avoided by comparing the *CUR*
of various population groups that have the same earnings capacity.
For example, rather than comparing the *CUR* of the average black
man with that of the average white man (as in the top half of Table
3.2), we can compare the *CUR* of the average black man having an
earnings capacity of $X with that of the average white man *having
the same earnings capacity*. These "earnings capacity constant"
CUR estimates, shown in the bottom half Table 3.2, and are referred
to as adjusted *CUR* (*ACUR*) estimates. They are obtained by statistically holding earnings capacity constant when comparing utilization
among groups.[8]

The utilization patterns suggested by *ACUR* differ from the
observed rates in the top half of the table. In particular, the racial

comparison is reversed: The *ACUR* of nonaged black units (70%) exceeds that of nonaged white units (64%) when both are evaluated at the mean earnings capacity for the total nonaged population. Similarly, while black men have a lower *CUR* than white men, the *ACUR* is equal for the two groups. Indeed, the *ACUR* is higher for single black men than for single white men—74% compared to 68%. The patterns described earlier for married and single men and women are not significantly altered by moving from *CUR* to *ACUR*.[9] Nor is the comparison between all black women and all white women altered. The difference between the *ACUR* for married black women and that for married white women, however, is smaller than the comparable difference in the *CUR*. On the other hand, the *ACUR* is actually higher for black female heads and single women than for white female heads and single women.

The comparison of *CUR* and *ACUR* in Table 3.2 indicates a positive relationship between earnings capacity and rates of capacity utilization. In Table 3.3, this relationship is explored for the nonaged population stratified by marital status, sex, and race. The table presents estimates of capacity utilization rates for each population group at each decile of the group's distribution of earnings capacity.[10]

[8] The *ACUR* estimates were obtained from the following regression:

$$E = a_0 + a_1 GEC + a_2 GEC^2 + a_3 GEC^3 + a_4 St + a_5 X,$$

where E is earnings, St is a 0–1 variable indicating student status, and X is a dummy variable indicating the comparison within group desired. The coefficient on the dummy variable indicates the effect of that variable on earnings, holding *GEC* constant. Separate regressions were run for all subgroups indicated in the stub of Table 3.1. In addition, separate regressions by race were run. Each regression was evaluated at the mean *GEC* of the larger group to which its observations belonged (all families and individuals, all men, or all women). The resulting estimate of E was placed over the corresponding value of *GEC* to obtain the *ACUR* for the desired subgroups, *holding earnings capacity constant.*

[9] The *ACUR* estimates in Table 3.2 are adjusted only for differences in marital status and race within sex groups. They are not adjusted for differences in earnings capacity between sex groups. The relationship between men and women observed in Table 3.2 is not altered when such adjustments are made.

[10] These estimates are obtained from the regressions of earnings on earnings capacity described in footnote 8. As indicated there, separate regressions are run on each subgroup. Each regression is evaluated at the deciles of the *GEC* distribution for the major population groups, and the resulting estimate of earnings at each decile is placed over the corresponding value of *GEC* to obtain the capacity utilization rate at that decile.

Table 3.3

CAPACITY UTILIZATION RATES, BY MARITAL STATUS, SEX, RACE, AND EARNINGS CAPACITY: NONAGED POPULATION

Decile of earnings capacity distribution	Families and individuals			Married population			Men			Women		
	Total	White	Black	Total	White	Black	Total	White	Black	Total	White	Black
10%	56	56	44	64	63	66	80	80	76	35	33	43
20%	60	61	53	64	63	68	81	81	78	34	33	43
30%	63	63	59	64	63	70	82	82	80	33	32	43
40%	64	64	61	64	64	70	83	83	81	33	31	44
50%	64	65	64	65	64	71	84	85	82	32	31	45
60%	65	65	66	65	65	70	86	86	83	32	31	45
70%	65	65	68	65	65	70	87	87	83	32	31	46
80%	66	66	69	66	66	69	89	89	83	32	31	47
90%	66	66	70	67	67	68	92	93	84	31	31	48

Decile of earnings capacity distribution	Married men			Single men			Married women			Single women		
	Total	White	Black	Total	White	Black	Total	White	Black	Total	White	Black
10%	84	84	82	57	57	63	35	32	46	37	37	38
20%	84	84	84	60	59	64	32	30	46	40	41	37
30%	85	85	85	62	62	65	31	29	46	43	46	38
40%	85	86	85	64	64	66	29	28	46	46	47	40
50%	86	87	86	66	66	67	29	27	46	48	50	41
60%	88	88	86	68	68	68	28	26	46	51	52	43
70%	89	89	87	70	70	69	27	25	46	55	55	46
80%	90	91	87	72	73	70	26	25	45	58	58	49
90%	94	95	87	75	76	71	24	24	44	62	63	54

NOTE: Values expressed as percentages.

As the first column of the table indicates, within the total nonaged population, capacity utilization increases steadily with earnings capacity from 56% at the first decile to 66% at the ninth. This pattern holds for whites and blacks considered separately, although the relationship is stronger for blacks than for whites. But this relationship is much less pronounced for the married population than it is for the total population. Although capacity utilization among all husband–wife units does increase with earnings capacity, the increase is very small—from 64% at the first decile to 67% at the ninth. Moreover, within the black married population, the relationship is not monotonic; rather it is like an inverted U.

The overall patterns of family capacity utilization mask some interesting differences between married men and married women. While capacity utilization is positively related to earnings capacity for married men—varying from 84% at the first decile to 94% at the ninth—the pattern for married women is reversed. The capacity utilization rate of nonaged wives *decreases* uniformly from 35% at the first decile of earnings capacity to 24% at the ninth. These patterns are found among both blacks and whites. Assuming that the capacities of husbands and wives are positively related, the division of market work effort between husbands and wives appears to depend upon family earnings capacity. As one moves up the distribution of family earnings capacity, the differences in utilization by husbands and wives offset one another, yielding the virtually flat relationship between capacity utilization and earnings capacity.

In contrast to this virtually flat relationship within the married population, the relationship of utilization to capacity is positive and steep within the unmarried male and the female populations, though the relationship is somewhat weaker for black single men than for white. Again, this relationship may be somewhat exaggerated for the single population. As suggested previously, physical and mental disabilities not captured by our data may cause our estimates of the earnings capacity of single men and women to be biased upward, and this bias is also likely to be more severe for low-capacity individuals. A mentally retarded individual, for example, is more likely to be single. Moreover, because of low education he will have a low estimated earnings capacity. To be sure, most people with little or no education are not mentally retarded, and many have substantial earnings; but because our data do not distinguish among mental abilities within the group of those with low estimated earnings capacity, true earnings capacity will be below estimated earnings capacity. Finally, this strong relationship may, in part, be caused by differences in demand between high-skill and low-skill workers. While our estimates of capacity are adjusted for reported weeks of unemployment, they are not adjusted either for the part-time work that results from this differential in demand or for the labor force withdrawals prompted by the unavailability of work.

Even if these possible biases were eliminated, however, this relationship between capacity and its utilization would, in all likelihood, remain. Among female heads of households, for example, welfare programs will tend to be more attractive to those with low earnings capacity than to those with high earnings capacity. Hence female heads with low earnings capacity will tend to substitute program income for earnings, implying a lower rate of capacity utilization. In general, the lower a person's earnings capacity, the less attractive from both monetary and nonmonetary standpoints are available jobs.

To summarize, among the nonaged population as a whole, capacity utilization increases steadily with earnings capacity. However, most of this increase is attributable to the relatively steep relationship between utilization and earnings capacity within the single population. For married units, the relationship of utilization to capacity is virtually flat. The positive relationship between capacity and its utilization for married men tends to be offset by a negative relationship for married women.

Given these results, what can be concluded regarding the relationship between low income and capacity utilization for blacks and other groups with a high incidence of poverty as measured by income? First, as indicated in Table 3.2, the difference between the *CUR* of blacks and that of whites is very small. Moreover, with earnings capacity held constant, black families have a somewhat higher rate of utilization than white families. Hence, racial differences in earnings cannot be attributed to racial differences in the utilization of earnings capacity.

Our results also indicate that low utilization of earnings capacity plays a relatively minor role in explaining the general problem of poverty. The differences in capacity utilization between families of low and high economic status are swamped by differences in earnings capacity between these types of families. The ratio of the utilization rates of those at the first and ninth decile is .87; the comparable ratio of earnings capacities is .27. This contrast is even more clear among the nonaged married population: while those at the lowest decile have virtually the same utilization rates as those at the highest decile, those at the lowest have less than one-half the earnings capacity of those at the highest. This evidence provides no support for the hypothesis that the high incidence of poverty among blacks and other population subgroups is primarily attributable to their failure to exploit economic potential.[11]

Earnings Capacity and Economic Inequality

The observed variation in the utilization of earnings capacity contributes to the inequality observed in the distribution of pre-transfer income (PTY). Indeed, if the degree of capacity utilization were constant for all units, the distributions of PTY and earnings capacity would display the same degree of inequality. Since we have ascertained that capacity utilization does vary systematically with earnings capacity, it is clear that the distribution of PTY will be more unequal than the distribution of earnings capacity. In this section, various measures of inequality based on income and earnings capacity are assessed, and the relative contributions to observed income inequality of variations in earnings capacity and in the utilization of earnings capacity are estimated.

Studies of the income distribution have relied on annually released statistics prepared by the United States Bureau of the Census and based upon the annual March Current Population Survey (see, for example, Morgan *et al.* 1962; Taussig 1973; U.S. Bureau of the Census 1973). Two basic findings have resulted from these studies. First, there is a substantial degree of inequality in current family money income in the United States. For example, the income level of the top fifth of American families is more than eight times that of the bottom fifth (see Miller 1966; Taussig 1973). Second, since the end of World War II, the degree of income inequality in the United States

[11] It should be emphasized that even if the CUR of blacks were below that of whites, it could not necessarily be concluded that whites use their capacities more fully than blacks. An alternative interpretation would be that, for reasons of either supply or demand (for example, labor market discrimination in the quantity of work offered), the economy fails to utilize the capacities of blacks as fully as those of whites.

has not changed markedly. The war resulted in a significant narrowing of the distribution, but since the war its structure has been virtually fixed.

As emphasized in Chapter 1, both the concepts and the data that underlie such studies of inequality have substantial weaknesses. Perhaps the primary weakness is the limited nature of the income concept employed: Although the real economic welfare of a family is related to both its potential real consumption over some period of time and its size, the conventional income concept includes only a fraction of the flows that compose this value. For example, all nonmoney income receipts are excluded from the concept, as are the consumption values of leisure, net worth, and capital gains. As a result, studies of inequality based on this concept are subject to the biases these weaknesses imply—in particular, the transitory forces that are reflected in the concept of current income.

The indicator of economic status that we call earnings capacity differs significantly from the conventional concept of family income. This indicator reflects the ability of a family to generate economic returns (money income) rather than the extent to which it actually does generate such returns. In effect, it takes the income-generating structure of the economy—labor markets and capital markets—as fixed and inquires into what the value of the full set of human and physical assets possessed by a family would be if these were used to capacity to generate income. In essence, this indicator of status focuses on the economic potential (or the economic capability) of a family unit, while conventional analyses of income distribution focus on the extent to which a family does in fact realize this capability.

We now turn to the data to compare the various measures of inequality. First, the degree of inequality in economic status as represented by measured inequality in the distributions of gross and net earnings capacity ($\widetilde{GEC}^*$ and $\widetilde{NEC}^*$) is presented.[12] These estimates of inequality in economic status are compared with estimates of inequality in the income distribution. Figures on inequality are provided for both the total population and the nonaged population. While numerous measures of inequality are available, we employ data on the shares of income (or earnings capacity) going to each income (earnings capacity) class, the standard Lorenz curve, and the

[12] Because the analysis in this section requires a comparison of the degree of variation in the observations within distributions, the randomized estimates of the earnings capacity variables are required. As Chapter 2 indicates, the nonrandomized estimates artificially compress the degree of variation in the distribution of earnings capacity.

Table 3.4

DISTRIBUTION OF INCOME AND EARNINGS CAPACITY BY QUINTILE, TOTAL POPULATION

	Economic status indicator			
Quintile	Pretransfer income	Total family income	$\widetilde{GEC}^*$	$\widetilde{NEC}^*$
Bottom 10%	.6	1.4	1.4	1.4
0–20%	1.6	3.5	3.5	3.5
20–40%	4.5	7.3	7.4	7.3
40–60%	11.0	14.3	14.3	14.3
60–80%	25.6	26.6	26.7	26.6
80–100%	57.3	48.3	48.2	48.2
Gini coefficient	.557	.456	.455	.455

NOTE: Values are expressed in percentages.

Gini coefficient.[13] Finally, differences in income and earnings capacity inequality are attributed to the varying patterns of capacity utilization described in the previous section.

In Table 3.4, estimates are presented of the shares of pretransfer income, total family income, gross earnings capacity ($\widetilde{GEC}^*$), and net earnings capacity ($\widetilde{NEC}^*$) accruing to the poorest through the richest segments of the total United States population. The last row presents the Gini coefficients for these measures of economic status. Figure 3.1 displays the Lorenz curves for the four distributions of economic status.[14]

[13] The Lorenz curve depicts graphically the cumulative share of income (or earnings capacity) going to successively larger proportions of the population. Percentage of consumer units cumulated from lowest to highest income (or earnings capacity) is measured along the horizontal axis, while percentage of income (or earnings capacity) cumulated from lowest to highest is measured along the vertical axis. The 45° line drawn from the southwest to the northeast of such a graph is called the line of perfect equality, since points along it indicate that the bottom 10% receive 10% of total income (earnings capacity), the bottom 30% receive 30% of total income, and so forth. The greater the area between the Lorenz curve and the 45° line of equality, the greater the degree of inequality. The Gini coefficient is the ratio of this area to the entire area in the triangle under the equality line.

The weaknesses of these and other descriptive statistics that describe entire distributions are discussed in Bronfenbrenner (1971). (See also Atkinson 1970.)

[14] The technique employed in estimating the Lorenz curve and the Gini coefficient for each of the distributions of economic status is based on that developed in Kakwani and Podder (1973); this method is described in Appendix A.

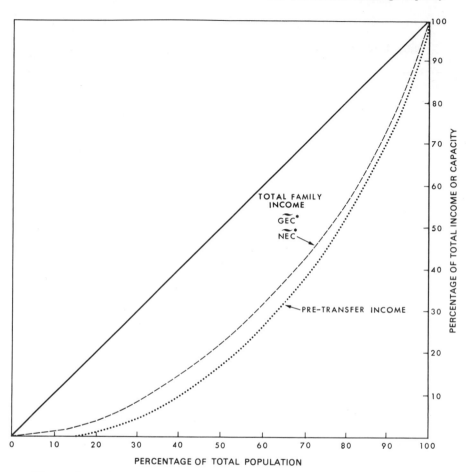

Figure 3.1. Lorenz curves of income and earnings capacity, total population. The curves for total family income, $\widehat{GEC}^*$, and $\widehat{NEC}^*$ are so close that they are indistinguishable on this graph.

The degree of inequality implicit in all of the indicators of economic status is substantial. In each case, the lowest 20% of the families account for less than 4% of aggregate income or earnings capacity, while the top 20% account for at least 48%. Moreover, as expected, inequality in the distribution of pretransfer income is substantially higher than inequality in total family income. For example, the poorest 20% of the population gets only 1.6% of pretransfer income, but 3.5% of total family income. While the Gini coefficient for pretransfer income is .557, that for total family income is .456. Similarly, the Lorenz curve for total family income lies well within the curve for pretransfer income. Finally, the degree of inequality in the two indicators of earnings capacity ($G\widetilde{E}C^*$ and $N\widetilde{E}C^*$) is almost identical and is equal to the degree of inequality in the distribution of total family income. In each case, the share going to the poorest 20% of the nation's families is 3.5%. In each case, the Gini coefficient is .455, and it is impossible to distinguish among the three Lorenz curves.[15]

It is clear from the data in Table 3.4 that differences in capacities account for the bulk of inequality in the United States distribution of income. The inequality present in the distribution of earnings capacity is 80% as great as the inequality in pretransfer income. Hence, at most one-fifth of the inequality in the distribution of pretransfer income can be attributed to differences in the taste for income rather than leisure, the effects of transfer programs on labor supply, or the impediments to labor market activity caused by the expenses required for working (primarily child care costs)—the factors that account for the variation in capacity utilization.[16]

In Table 3.5 and Figure 3.2 we present the same income distribution measures as those presented in Table 3.4 and Figure 3.1, but for the nonaged population. The inequality of distribution among the nonaged population is similar to that among the total population. Again, irrespective of the measure of economic status, inequality is substantial. In each case, the lowest 20% of the families account for less than 4% of aggregate income or earnings capacity, while the top 20% account for about 50%. Moreover, inequality in the distribution

[15] For purposes of comparison, inequality in the distribution of welfare ratios is also estimated for the four measures of economic status. Through this procedure, the degree of inequality of status relative to needs can be appraised. In general, the welfare ratio Gini coefficients are similar to the Gini coefficients shown in Table 3.4. Two differences, however, are notable. First, $G\widetilde{E}C^*$ welfare ratios are much less unequally distributed than $G\widetilde{E}C^*$, while this is not the case for $N\widetilde{E}C^*$. Second, the Gini coefficients for welfare ratios are uniformly smaller than those for the comparable nondeflated measures; the distribution of economic resources in relation to needs among the nonaged population is less unequal than the distribution of actual income or earnings capacity.

[16] A comparison between earnings capacity and pretransfer income rather than total family income is, in general, more appropriate for addressing the issue of the effect of differences in taste or labor supply responses on the income distribution. While the earnings capacity measures indicate what income flows families could generate if they made the full capacity services of their human and physical assets available to the market, the pretransfer income variable indicates what flows families *do* in fact generate from their labor and capital market activities.

Table 3.5

DISTRIBUTION OF INCOME AND EARNINGS CAPACITY BY QUINTILE,
NONAGED POPULATION

	Economic status indicator			
Quintile	Pretransfer income	Total family income	$\widetilde{GEC}^*$	$\widetilde{NEC}^*$
Bottom 10%	.7	1.2	1.5	.8
0–20%	1.9	3.0	3.7	2.2
20–40%	4.9	6.7	7.5	5.5
40–60%	11.6	13.6	14.5	12.3
60–80%	25.9	26.6	26.7	26.2
80–100%	55.7	50.2	47.7	53.9
Gini coefficient	.540	.479	.448	.521
	(.557)	(.456)	(.455)	(.455)

NOTE: Values are expressed in percentages. Figures in parentheses are Gini coefficients for the total population.

of pretransfer income is larger than inequality in the distribution of total family income. The Gini coefficient is .540 for pretransfer income and .479 for total family income.

Several differences between the total and nonaged populations in the degree of inequality do exist, however, and should be pointed out. First, a comparison of the Gini coefficients for total family income and $\widetilde{NEC}^*$ suggests that economic status may be somewhat more unequally distributed among the nonaged population than among the total population. The Gini coefficient for family income is .456 for the total population and .479 for the nonaged population. The Gini coefficients for $\widetilde{NEC}^*$ are .455 and .521 for the two groups. Second, because of these differences, the rank order of the indicators is altered in moving from the total to the nonaged population. In particular, while the Gini coefficients for $\widetilde{GEC}^*$, $\widetilde{NEC}^*$, and total family income are nearly identical for the total population, the Gini coefficients for $\widetilde{NEC}^*$ and total family income increase substantially and that for $\widetilde{GEC}^*$ falls slightly in moving to the nonaged population. The reasons for these changes are clear:

1. Because older families (with few if any children) are excluded in the nonaged population, the child care adjustment in $\widetilde{NEC}^*$ has a more potent impact in reducing the relative economic status of low-

capacity families than of high-capacity families—given the relatively larger family sizes of low-capacity families.

2. The fact that Social Security and pension transfers have little impact on the nonaged population and that their equalizing effect is not recorded for that group, raises the Gini coefficient on total family income for the nonaged population relative to the total population. For the same region, the gap between the Gini coefficients on pretransfer and total family income is narrowed from .101 for the total population to .061 for the nonaged population.

Again, the degree of inequality in pretransfer income attributable to variations in earnings capacity as opposed to variations in utiliza-

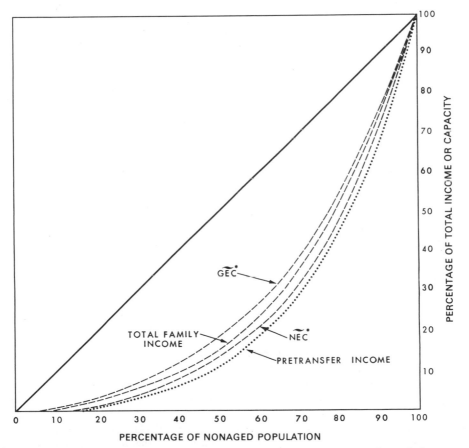

Figure 3.2. Lorenz curves of income and earnings capacity, nonaged population.

tion of earnings capacity can be identified. Comparing the Gini coefficient for pretransfer income to that for $\widehat{GEC}^*$ suggests that variation in earnings capacity accounts for the bulk of the inequality in market-related income. Since the Gini coefficients for $\widehat{GEC}^*$ is 82% as great as that for pretransfer income, about 18% of the inequality in pretransfer income can be attributed to variation in utilization of earnings capacity.

A final comparison of Gini coefficients allows those factors that account for the variation in utilization of capacity—and, hence, for 18% of the inequality in pretransfer income—to be crudely decomposed. Because the distributions of both $\widehat{NEC}^*$ and pretransfer income reflect the primary component of the real costs of labor market activity (namely, child care costs), a comparison of these two measures tends to capture the effect on the inequality in pretransfer income of remaining sources of variation in utilization of capacity— namely, tastes for work versus leisure and labor supply reductions induced by transfer programs. The ratio of the Gini coefficients for $\widehat{NEC}^*$ (.521) and pretransfer income (.540) is .96, which suggests that about 4% of the inequality in pretransfer income is attributable to the effect of these other factors on utilization of capacity. Hence, the real costs of labor market activity are estimated to account for about 14% of the observed inequality in pretransfer income (the difference between 18% and 4%).[17] It should be emphasized, however, that the child care impediments to labor force activity are rather differently reflected in PTY and $\widehat{NEC}^*$. Hence, this residual of 14% must be interpreted as a very crude estimate of the effect of tastes and labor supply responses on the inequality in the distribution of pretransfer income.

Conclusions

These empirical results shed light on a number of important issues regarding the causes of poverty and the determinants of income inequality. While some of them confirm ex ante expectations, others fail to verify propositions that appear to be widely believed. Some of the primary conclusions can be summarized as follows:

[17] Note, however, that these results suggest that part of the inequality in pretransfer income may be due to differences in the taste for children that lead to differences in the utilization of gross earnings capacities.

- For the entire nonaged population, the utilization of economic capacity is relatively high—nearly 65%. This rate varies from 87% for nonaged males to 52% for female household heads and 27% for wives. The rates for wives and female heads would be substantially higher if the full value of nonmarket work were imputed to those who are not full-time, full-year workers. When a crude estimate of the market value of the child care services they provide is added to their market earnings, the utilization rate for all women increases from 33% to 44%.
- Although the *observed* capacity utilization rate is slightly lower for black families than for white families, this differential is accounted for by the high earnings capacity of whites relative to blacks. When black and white families *of the same earnings capacity* are compared, black families have higher rates of capacity utilization than white families for most earnings capacity levels.
- Similarly, while the capacity utilization rates of poor households are slightly lower than those of households of high economic status, this difference is primarily attributable to the capacity utilization patterns of unmarried persons. For families, the rates of capacity utilization are nearly constant over the distribution of economic status.
- The contribution of differences in capacity utilization to income inequality is small. The distribution of earnings capacity is about four-fifths as unequal as the distribution of pretransfer income indicating that at most one-fifth of observed income inequality is attributable to differences in capacity utilization.[18] In turn, child care expenses (the primary real cost of labor market activity) appear to account for about two-thirds of the variation in capacity utilization and, hence, for about 14% of the inequality in pretransfer income.

[18] This conclusion is subject to two, offsetting biases. First, our randomization procedure assumes that all differences in earnings among individuals except those attributable to deviations from full-time, full-year work reflect differences in capacity. Measured and unmeasured human capital differences, sectoral demand factors, and exogenous random events are treated as capacity related effects. To the extent that a portion of the variance due to these factors is attributed to choice, the estimated contribution of capacity differences to observed inequality is overstated. Second, part of the variation attributed to choice may be due to unmeasured human capital characteristics. This would occur if the deviation from full-time, full-year work is positively correlated with these unmeasured characteristics. For example, the true earnings capacity of non-labor-force participants is likely to be less than that of labor force participants with the same measured characteristics, but our measure of earnings capacity for the two groups would not reflect this difference.

4

Earnings Capacity and Poverty

In this chapter, we develop a definition of poverty based on the concept of earnings capacity. Using this definition, we identify the demographic composition of the poor population and compare it to the composition of the poor population according to the standard definition of poverty. Finally, looking at both definitions, we compare and contrast the independent contributions of various socioeconomic characteristics—age, sex, race, education, family size—to the probability of being poor.

The Earnings Capacity Poor and the Current Income Poor

Placing both the earnings capacity and the current income measures of family economic status over the 1973 poverty line for a family yields "welfare ratios" based on both current income and earnings capacity for each family.[1] By employing these welfare ratios, we can determine and compare the composition of both the current income and earnings capacity poverty populations.

According to the official definition of poverty, an individual is poor if he or she lives in a family in which the ratio of current income to welfare is less than unity. By this conventional definition, about 11% of the total United States population were poor in 1973. If this percentage is accepted as a benchmark, an equivalent number of individuals in families with the lowest ratios of earnings capacity to welfare can be isolated and the composition of the two groups compared. To the extent that earnings capacity captures important characteristics of economic status that are not reflected in current money income, we gain information about the nature of the poor population from this comparison. Because of the nature of the concept, the poor population defined by earnings capacity will include more individuals with low permanent income than will the poor population based on the temporally unstable concept of current money income.

Although analyses of the composition of the poor population typically use households as the unit of measurement, this analysis focuses on individuals.[2] Households are not of inherent value in themselves but only as aggregates of individuals. Clearly, if all households were of equal size, the household and the individual would be interchangeable units of measurement. However, if all people are to be treated equally, a household of 10 poor individuals must be of more concern than a household of but 1 poor individual. Similarly, eliminating poverty in a household of 10 individuals is more of an accomplishment than moving a household with a single individual over the poverty threshold. As we will see, the picture presented by data on the composition of the poor in terms of households is quite different from that presented by data on poor individuals—and, perhaps, is misleading.

[1] The 1973 poverty lines for urban families are officially designated as follows: family size 1, $2475; family size 2, $3095; family size 3, $3720; and so on. In addition to variation by family size, the poverty line is somewhat lower for rural families. See Orshansky (1965) for a discussion of the concept of a poverty threshold. The concept and use of the welfare ratio originated in the research of Morgan *et al.* (1962).

[2] To obtain the composition of the poor population, we first classified persons as poor or nonpoor on the basis of the income or earnings capacity of their households. The poor individuals were then aggregated into categories on the basis of the socioeconomic characteristics of the heads of their households.

In Table 4.1 data on the composition of current income and earnings capacity poor individuals are presented, as well as data on the composition of current income poor *households*. This table includes all poor individuals in the population. Two measures of earnings capacity are used ($\widetilde{NEC}^*$ and $\widetilde{GEC}^*$) both of which reflect the randomization procedure described in Chapter 2. The latter measure is included so that compositional differences attributable only to the child care adjustment can be identified.[3]

Examining the composition of current income (CY) poor households and individuals, we see that data on households lead to a serious overstatement of the proportion of the poor who live in small households and, as a consequence, the proportion of the poor who are aged and who live in families with no earners. Measuring poverty in terms of households also understates, though less dramatically, the proportions of the CY poor who are black and live in the South.

Differences between the composition of CY poor individuals and that of earnings capacity (EC) poor individuals are equally striking. Moreover, they reinforce the compositional differences between CY poverty measured by households and CY poverty measured by individuals.

Perhaps the most striking difference in composition between EC and CY poverty is in work status. While only 26% of the CY poor live in households in which the head works 50–52 weeks, 40% of the $\widetilde{NEC}^*$ poor live in such households. This difference in work status is easily explained. Current income is closely related to the number of workers in a household and how much each of them works. Earnings capacity is not directly related to either of these variables. Consequently, while families with two earners are unlikely to have current income sufficiently low to place them below the poverty threshold, such families may well have ratios of earnings capacity to welfare that place them at the very bottom of the distribution of earnings capacity.

---

[3] While deflation of the net earnings capacity measures by the poverty lines might appear to entail a double adjustment for children, it does not. The poverty lines are dependent on family size and rural–urban residence and are designed to reflect the level of need for families of various sizes and locations. The child care adjustment for calculating net earnings capacity is designed to reflect the necessary costs incurred by a family with children if both the head and spouse (or only the head, if no spouse is present) work at full-time, full-year jobs. It is not related to any judgment regarding need.

Table 4.1

DISTRIBUTION OF EARNINGS CAPACITY AND CURRENT INCOME POOR
INDIVIDUALS AND HOUSEHOLDS, BY SOCIOECONOMIC CHARACTERISTICS:
TOTAL POPULATION

	$\widetilde{NEC}^*$	$\widetilde{GEC}^*$	Current income	
	individuals	individuals	Individuals	Households
Race of head				
White	59.96	60.90	67.70	76.37
Black	38.34	37.28	30.82	22.56
Other	1.70	1.81	1.33	1.33
Sex of head				
Male	49.88	40.57	45.60	45.95
Female	50.12	59.43	54.40	54.05
Age of head				
16–21	2.38	2.35	4.69	6.75
22–30	21.53	14.35	17.07	13.60
31–40	29.47	21.76	22.62	12.06
41–50	19.93	20.01	17.37	11.27
51–60	10.92	14.68	12.66	12.46
61–64	2.80	4.45	4.70	6.61
65 or more	12.96	22.41	20.87	37.26
Family size				
1	6.25	13.99	19.29	48.67
2	6.26	11.40	14.64	18.47
3–4	22.94	23.30	22.06	16.04
5–6	28.35	23.51	20.54	9.57
7–8	21.16	17.10	15.25	5.23
9 or more	15.24	10.17	8.22	2.02
Education of head				
0–8	46.71	51.23	48.94	49.53
9–12	47.76	42.37	41.65	38.19
13–16	5.23	5.46	8.36	10.81
17 or more	.31	.44	1.06	1.47
Occupation of head				
Professional	3.60	3.96	3.44	5.27
Farmer	2.95	2.65	12.84	11.13
Manager	5.12	4.97	8.15	8.14
Clerical	9.53	12.77	5.13	8.36
Sales	2.59	2.87	2.96	3.81
Craftsman	13.70	11.33	9.60	7.96
Operative	26.57	24.26	16.97	13.47
Private household	5.13	6.50	8.66	6.46

Table 4.1   (Continued)

	$\widetilde{NEC}^*$ individuals	$\widetilde{GEC}^*$ individuals	Current income Individuals	Households
Service	15.68	18.00	17.34	15.55
Farm laborer	5.21	4.84	6.53	7.93
Laborer	9.90	7.84	9.33	10.96
Region				
Northeast	17.41	18.44	15.72	18.29
North Central	21.49	21.12	22.61	24.57
South	46.44	46.12	46.24	40.78
West	14.66	14.20	15.42	16.36
Location				
Town	15.92	16.63	13.99	15.12
Rural	4.47	35.07	40.58	34.25
Suburb	15.84	15.10	14.44	16.73
Central city	33.77	33.20	30.99	33.90
Number of earners				
0	27.28	33.70	42.18	54.94
1	52.63	50.33	45.02	37.69
2	20.09	15.97	12.81	7.37
Weeks worked (head)				
0	28.34	35.27	43.65	55.91
1–13	7.43	8.00	9.58	9.70
14–26	7.68	7.84	7.99	7.69
27–39	7.82	7.58	6.58	4.95
40–47	6.40	5.42	4.58	3.00
48–49	2.87	1.90	1.70	1.12
50–52	39.45	34.00	25.92	17.63
Work (head)				
Full time	83.44	79.86	73.44	65.84
Part time	16.56	20.14	26.56	34.16

NOTE: Values are expressed in percentages.

It should also be noted that the proportion of the poor in families with workers is higher among the $\widetilde{NEC}^*$ poor than among the $\widetilde{GEC}^*$ poor. This is largely attributable to the child care adjustment, which reduces the $\widetilde{NEC}^*$ of the nonaged population relative to that of the aged population. The former are much more likely to have children; the latter are much less likely to live in households with workers.

A second striking difference between the compositions of the *CY* poor and the *EC* poor is in racial composition. Whereas 31% of *CY* poor individuals are black (and fewer than one-quarter of *CY* poor households are black), about 38% of the *EC* poor are black.[4] The current income measure of economic status understates the low economic status of blacks relative to whites. This is largely caused by the much higher labor force participation rate and hours worked of black wives.

The differences by sex of head are not nearly so dramatic; in fact, the difference in composition between the $\widetilde{GEC}^*$ poor and the $\widetilde{NEC}^*$ poor is larger than the difference between either of them and the composition of the *CY* poor. The proportion of poor individuals in families headed by males increases in moving from $\widetilde{GEC}^*$ to $\widetilde{NEC}^*$, largely because intact (male-headed) families have more children, on average, than do single-parent families.

More striking is the effect of the child care deduction on the proportion of poor individuals by the age of the family head. While 21% of the *CY* poor and 22% of the $\widetilde{GEC}^*$ poor live in families with heads who are 65 years old or older, only 13% of the $\widetilde{NEC}^*$ poor live in such families. (Again note that the difference between the age composition of *CY* poor households and $\widetilde{NEC}^+$ poor individuals is even more dramatic—37% as opposed to 13%.) If $\widetilde{NEC}^*$ is the preferred measure of economic status, the standard poverty measure appears to overstate the proportion of older people in the poverty population. On the other hand, it should be noted that, since unhealthy aged individuals are much less likely to give health as their reason for not working than unhealthy younger individuals, the estimates of $\widetilde{GEC}^*$ and $\widetilde{NEC}^*$ for the aged may be somewhat overstated.

Even without the deduction for child care, the difference in family size composition between the *EC* poor and the *CY* poor is notable. Far fewer *EC* poor persons are single, and more have large families. Whereas almost 20% of *CY* poor individuals (49% of *CY* poor households) live alone, only 14% of the $\widetilde{GEC}^*$ poor and 6% of the $\widetilde{NEC}^*$ poor live alone. Indeed, more than 15% of the $\widetilde{NEC}^*$ poor live in families with nine or more members (10% without the child care adjustment), while only 8% of the *CY* poor live in such large families.[5]

[4] Blacks make up only about 11% of the total population.

[5] The stronger effect of family size on the probability of *EC* poverty relative to *CY* poverty is, in part, attributable to the differential treatment by these two measures of

Another interesting difference is between the proportions of *EC* and *CY* poor who live in families headed by farmers: 13% of the *CY* poor, but only 3% of the *EC* poor. This difference suggests that most farmers who are poor by the current income measure have sufficient human capital to do better economically if they were willing to leave their farms. Our measure of human capital is imperfect, however. In particular, what individuals could earn if they switched occupations and locations late in life may not be accurately measured. Because of this, the earnings capacity of at least some older farmers may be overstated. In any case, the small proportion of *EC* poor who live in families headed by farmers is offset by the larger proportion who live in families headed by operatives (26% versus 17% of the *CY* poor), craftsmen (14% versus 10%) and clerical workers (10% versus 5%).

Some other differences are worth noting. The figures in Table 4.1 also indicate that a greater proportion of the *EC* poor than of the *CY* poor live in families whose heads have fewer than 12 years of schooling and a somewhat greater proportion live in central cities and in small towns.

To summarize, if our estimate of earnings capacity is superior to current income as an indicator of economic status, the use of the current income measure understates the proportion of the poorest 11% of the population who are black, who live in families headed by persons with low levels of education, who live in very large families, who live in households with one or more full time workers, whose

---

earners other than the head and spouse. While the numerator of the current income to welfare ratio for a family includes the contribution of such workers to family income, the numerator of the earnings capacity to welfare ratio does not include their contribution to earnings capacity. Because the probability that such earners will be present in a family is related to family size, the incidence of large families in *EC* poverty is biased upward relative to the incidence of such families in *CY* poverty. To test the potential importance of this bias, we ran another *CY* poverty regression with a variable for earnings of family members other than the head and spouse. The coefficient of this variable was negative and highly significant, and including it increased the coefficients of the large-family-size variables—7, 8, and 9 or more—from about 9, 10, and 7 to about 11, 16, and 10 respectively. Thus most of the differential remained. In addition, after the actual earnings of other family members were added to the numerator of our earnings capacity measure, the family size coefficients in the earnings capacity regression remained virtually unchanged. From these results we conclude that very little of the differential effects of family size on *CY* and *EC* poverty status is attributable to the differential treatment of earners other than the head and spouse.

family heads are younger than age 65 or older than age 22 and are not farmers, and who do not live alone. Moreover, analyzing the composition of CY poverty using households rather than persons exacerbates these biases.

In the analysis of composition of the poor in Table 4.1, the earnings capacity measures used are those generated by the randomization process. The extent to which the observed differences between the EC and CY poverty composition is attributable to the randomization technique is summarized in Appendix B, where two additional sets of poverty composition data are presented, both based on the earnings capacity definition of poverty. One set uses a second random number generation process to verify that the difference in composition between the randomized EC and CY poor is not a chance happening arising out of the randomization process. The second set uses the expected value for a family rather than the expected value plus or minus a random shock. This is done to determine the extent to which observed differences between the composition of EC poverty and that of CY poverty are attributable to the randomization process.

The results of this exercise indicate that the differences in composition between the poverty populations defined by the two randomized EC estimates are negligible. Some small differences exist between the composition of the poor estimated by random estimation procedures and the composition estimated by nonrandom procedures. In general, the randomization procedure tends to reduce slightly the differences between the EC poor and the CY poor in terms of race, years of schooling, region, and family size. It causes modest increases in the differences in the proportion of the poor who live in families with no earners or with aged heads.

In addition, estimates are made of the composition of *nonaged* individuals who are poor according to the EC and CY indicators of economic status. These are summarized in Appendix C. Although 11% of the total population live in families classified as poor by the standard definition, they comprise only 9.9% of the population aged 64 or younger. In general, the compositional differences between EC poverty and CY poverty observed in the total population are also present in the nonaged population. The primary differences occur in the proportion of individuals living in families headed by women (50% for $N\widetilde{EC}^*$ and 44% for CY, relative to 50% and 54% for the total population), in families with one or two workers (78% for $N\widetilde{E}C^*$ and 68% for CY, relative to 73% and 58% for the total population), and in families headed by blacks (41% for $N\widetilde{E}C^*$ and 34% for CY, relative to 38% and 31% for the total population).

Determinants of Poverty Status Based on Earnings Capacity and Current Income

Although the comparisons in Table 4.1 are helpful in discerning how the composition of the poor population changes in moving from a definition of economic status based on current income to one based on earnings capacity, they can lead to faulty inferences regarding which variables are the most important determinants of poverty status under each definition. For example, to observe that individuals both with low education and in low-status, low-skill occupations are heavily represented in the poverty population gives no indication of the independent contribution of either education or occupation to the probability of being poor. These independent effects can be captured only by answering the question, "How does the probability of an individual being in poverty change if, say, his or her educational attainment changes while other characteristics related to poverty status remain unchanged?"

Through the use of multiple regression analysis, estimates can be obtained of the independent contributions of various socioeconomic characteristics to the probability of being in poverty. By specifying a regression equation with a 0–1 dependent variable representing the poverty–nonpoverty status of individual families and with family characteristics as independent variables, we can determine the relationship of changes in any one family characteristic to the probability of poverty status—holding other characteristics constant.

To summarize the independent effects of various variables on poverty status, we estimate regressions of this form for the total population for both the standard CY and the $N\widetilde{E}C^*$ definitions of poverty. The independent variables used in both regressions include the variables presented in Table 4.1 expressed in dummy variable form. In Table 4.2, the contribution of each of the variables to the

Table 4.2

EFFECT OF FAMILY CHARACTERISTICS ON THE
PROBABILITY OF EARNINGS CAPACITY AND CURRENT
INCOME POVERTY STATUS

	$\widehat{NEC}$* coefficient		Current income coefficient	
Race of head				
White	—	—	—	—
Black	13.95	(33.2)	11.0	(25.5)
Other	1.84	(1.6)	4.01	(3.3)
Sex of head				
Male	—	—	—	—
Female	30.42	(71.2)	12.79	(29.2)
Age of head				
16–21	10.96	(11.3)	13.94	(14.0)
22–25	12.15	(21.1)	3.91	(6.6)
25–35	7.82	(22.6)	2.97	(8.3)
35–45	—	—	—	—
45–55	.2	(.6)	−1.44	(4.0)
55–64	2.64	(5.7)	−2.97	(4.8)
65 or more	1.74	(3.1)	−11.81	(20.3)
Family size				
1	−19.71	(33.7)	5.57	(9.3)
2	−8.06	(19.0)	−2.3	(5.3)
3	−4.21	(10.4)	−1.89	(4.5)
4	—	—	—	—
5	3.44	(8.7)	1.4	(3.4)
6	7.48	(16.3)	2.82	(6.0)
7	13.98	(24.7)	8.99	(15.5)
8	21.91	(30.0)	10.04	(13.4)
9 or more	26.61	(40.0)	6.6	(9.7)
Education of head				
0–8	10.33	(24.2)	9.5	(21.6)
9–12	3.44	(9.9)	2.72	(7.6)
13–16	—	—	—	—
17 or more	−.46	(.8)	−.45	(.8)
Occupation of head				
Farmer	−.86	(1.1)	20.39	(24.2)
Manager	1.13	(2.2)	2.68	(5.2)
Professional	—	—	—	—
Clerical	−.18	(.3)	−4.38	(6.8)
Sales	1.18	(1.8)	.81	(1.2)

Table 4.2   (Continued)

	$\widehat{NEC}$* coefficient		Current income coefficient	
Craftsman	.01	(.0)	−1.53	(2.9)
Operative	1.34	(2.5)	−2.16	(3.9)
Private household	11.95	(7.8)	15.57	(10.0)
Service	1.3	(2.1)	1.06	(1.6)
Farm laborer	9.18	(7.6)	20.29	(16.4)
Laborer	.58	(.8)	2.24	(3.1)
Region				
Northeast	−.26	(.8)	−.93	(2.7)
North Central	—	—	—	—
South	3.66	(11.5)	3.76	(11.6)
West	.82	(2.2)	.25	(.7)
Location				
Town	2.54	(6.4)	1.6	(3.8)
Rural	2.26	(6.9)	3.31	(9.8)
Central city	.19	(.6)	.26	(.8)
Suburb	—	—	—	—
Weeks worked (head)				
0	—	—	—	—
1–13	8.21	(8.2)	10.57	(10.3)
14–26	2.51	(2.6)	−2.73	(.3)
27–39	.52	(.6)	−9.93	(10.6)
40–47	−5.34	(5.8)	−12.58	(13.3)
48–49	−5.21	(4.9)	−15.33	(14.3)
50 or more	−7.23	(9.3)	−16.16	(20.2)
Weeks worked (spouse)				
0	—	—	—	—
1–13	−1.38	(2.5)	−.44	(.8)
14–26	−1.65	(2.8)	−2.88	(4.8)
27–39	−2.77	(4.4)	−3.29	(5.1)
40–47	−2.56	(3.4)	−2.81	(3.6)
48–49	−3.28	(3.0)	−2.94	(2.6)
50 or more	−3.13	(7.0)	−2.2	(4.8)
Work (head)				
Full time	.58	(1.0)	−9.15	(14.8)
Part time	—	—	—	—
Work (spouse)				
Full time	.97	(2.4)	−2.90	(6.9)
Part time	—	—	—	—
Constant	−.40	(.6)	21.72	(31.4)
r^2	.31		.276	
f	445.4		368.9	

NOTE: t values appear in parentheses.

probability of poverty status is shown for both the CY and $\widetilde{NEC}^*$ definitions.[6]

Interpretation of the numbers in the coefficient columns is straightforward: they show the *change* in the probability of a family being in poverty caused by a hypothetical *change* in one characteristic, holding all other characteristics constant. For example, if the head of the family were black rather than white—all other characteristics remaining fixed—the probability of the family being in poverty would be 11 percentage points higher in the CY definition (33%) and about 14% percentage points higher in the $\widetilde{NEC}^*$ definition (14). Similarly, the probability of poverty status for a family with a number of characteristics different from the base characteristics is obtained by adding the percentage points in the coefficient column to the constant term of the regression. Thus, for a family with all the base characteristics except that the head is black (instead of white) and aged 16–21 (instead of 35–45), the probability of being in CY poverty is equal to 22% (the constant) plus 11% (the pertinent number for black) plus 13.94% (the pertinent number for age 16–21)—for a total probability of 46.94%.

Several interesting contrasts between the two regressions are observable. First, as suggested earlier, the relationship of work status to poverty status is much weaker under the EC definition of poverty than under the CY. Aside from the adjustment for weeks not worked because of health limitations or unemployment, the EC measure of economic status does not depend directly on work, while the CY measure of economic status is directly dependent on the amount of work. Moreover, a female family head is an important determinant of poverty status under both definitions but has a much more powerful effect under the EC definition. This is not surprising, given the fact that female-headed families typically have but one adult to

---

[6] The constant term in these regression equations expresses the probability that a family with the base characteristics will be included in the poverty group. For the $\widetilde{NEC}^*$ regression, the constant term is effectively zero; for the current income regression, the constant term is 22. The explanation for this discrepancy lies primarily with the "weeks worked" variable for which the category "zero weeks worked" was omitted. Because "weeks worked" has very important direct effects on current income but no direct effect on earnings capacity, omission of the category "zero weeks worked" increases the estimated probability that a family with the base characteristics will experience CY poverty status but does not affect the probability of EC poverty status. Hence a family with the base characteristics is estimated to have zero probability of being poor by the EC measure but a 22% probability of being poor by the CY measure.

contribute to total family earnings capacity. On the basis of this fact alone, one would expect to find a substantially higher proportion of female-headed families in the EC poverty population than in the CY poverty population. But, as indicated in Table 4.1, the proportion of poor families with female heads is approximately the same for the CY and the EC definitions. A large number of female-headed families with children are counted as CY poor because the family heads do not work. Such families form a high proportion of the EC poor not because the heads do not work but because, relative to the rest of the population, they would earn so little even if they worked at capacity.

Perhaps one of the most striking findings is the effect of age—particularly old age—on the probability of being poor according to the two definitions. The pattern of the age coefficients in the $\widetilde{NEC}^*$ regression can be explained primarily by the underlying relationship between age and wage rates that is common in the human capital literature. Wage rates rise gradually until late middle age, then gradually decline. An opposite pattern is present in the current income regression, which shows the probability of CY poverty decreasing with age—particularly after age 65. This results from old age insurance and disability insurance payments; an aged nonworker is less likely to be poor than a younger nonworker. Also, the large positive value on a family of one to some extent offsets the negative value on age in the current income definition.

Family size, while an important determinant of poverty under both definitions, is more important under the EC definition than under the CY definition—partly because of the different ways the two measures treat family earners other than the head and spouse. While the numerator of the CY welfare ratio for a family includes the contribution of such workers to family income, the numerator of the EC ratio does not include their contribution to earnings capacity. In other analyses, we have included the earnings of other adults in the measure of earnings capacity. Because this adjustment does not significantly reduce the coefficients on the family size variables in this regression, we conclude that overstatement of the importance on the family size variables in the EC regression caused by the differential treatment of earners other than the head and spouse is small.

The impact of occupation on poverty status under the two definitions should also be noted. Consistent with the results in Table 4.1, those in Table 4.2 indicate that being a farmer, a farm laborer, or, to a lesser extent, a household worker—holding other characteristics constant—substantially increases the probability of being in CY poverty relative to the probability of being in EC poverty.

The Probability of Poverty Status for Various Family Types

The data in Table 4.2 can readily be adapted to provide an estimate of the probability of CY and EC poverty status for various family types. In Table 4.3, several types of family units are characterized and the probability of each family type being in CY and EC poverty is indicated. These probability estimates suggest some substantial differences between the EC and CY poverty definitions in terms of what sorts of families are classified as poor. Some similarities are also suggested.

Members of female-headed black families, large rural southern families, and migrant worker families have the highest probabilities of being poor by both definitions—about .71, .45, and .50, respectively. Moreover, the probabilities of members of each of these family types being poor are very similar for both definitions. The similar probabilities for female heads are consistent with the previous observation that the bigger effect of female headship on EC poverty status than on CY poverty status approximately offsets the small effect of work status on EC poverty status. Similarly, the greater effects on EC poverty status of educational attainment and family size tend to offset the smaller effects of being a farm worker for members of large rural southern families and migrant worker families. Perhaps even more interesting than these similarities, however, are the differences between the EC and CY measures in the probabilities of being poor for members of the other four family types.

The most striking difference is in the probabilities of an unmarried, young student being poor by the two definitions. Whereas the probability is .41 that such a person will be poor by the CY measure, it is virtually zero by the EC measure. For members of this group, low income is clearly a temporary phenomenon. Moreover, it reflects a voluntary choice to postpone consumption in order to enhance future consumption. Hence, the EC measure reflects the

Table 4.3

PROBABILITY OF SEVERAL FAMILY TYPES BEING CLASSIFIED AS
EARNINGS CAPACITY AND CURRENT INCOME POOR

Family type	$\widetilde{NEC}$*	Current income
Black female head with children— "AFDC stereotype"[a]	.71	.72
Large rural southern family[b]	.42	.47
Migrant worker family[c]	.51	.50
Single youth—"independent student"[d]	.0	.41
Middle-aged midwestern farm family[e]	.05	.24
Elderly couple[f]	.04	.15
Large, male-headed, low education family—"working poor family"[g]	.21	.09

[a] Black, female head, age 35–45, education 9–12, family size 5, Northeast, central city, head worked 1–13 weeks part time, no spouse, private household.

[b] Black, male head, age 35–45, education 0–8, family size 8, South, rural, head worked 40–47 weeks full time, spouse a nonworker, farm worker.

[c] Black, male head, age 35–45, education 0–8, family size 7, West, rural, head worked 27–39 weeks full time, spouse worked 14–26 weeks full time, farm laborer.

[d] White, male head, age 16–21, education 12–16, family size 1, Northeast, central city, head worked 1–13 weeks full time, no spouse, laborer.

[e] White, male head, age 45–55, education 9–12, family size 6, North Central, rural, head worked 50+ weeks full time, spouse a nonworker, farmer.

[f] White, male head, age 65 or more, education <8, family size 2, North Central, central city, head worked 0 weeks, spouse a nonworker, craftsman.

[g] White, male head, age 35–45, education 9–12, family size 8, South, central city, head worked 50–52 weeks full time, spouse worked 14–26 weeks full time, laborer.

generally accepted judgment that the low income of these individuals is not nearly so pressing a social problem as the low incomes of other members of society.

The case of the middle-aged midwestern farm family is similar in some respects to that of the student. First, the probability that members of this family type will be poor by the EC measure is much lower—.05 versus .24—than the probability that they will be poor by the *CY* measure. Second, the relatively low income of some members of this group is attributable, at least in part, to their preference for farm life over town or city life. That is, many members of this group have estimated earnings capacities that exceed their actual incomes. How many of them could actually earn more if they left the farm and searched for jobs in towns or cities is not clear. Recall that our estimates of earnings capacity do not take into account the effect of particular kinds of previous job experience on current earnings abilities. Still, it seems clear that at least a portion of the observed *CY* poverty of farmers is voluntary.

As with the middle-aged farm family, there is some ambiguity in accounting for the different probabilities of being poor for the elderly couple. On the one hand, the lower probability of the elderly poor being counted among the *EC* poor than among the *CY* poor—.04 versus .15—is certainly attributable, at least in part, to the greater consumption of leisure by the aged than by the rest of the population. On the other hand, as noted earlier, the estimates of earnings capacity do not adequately reflect health disabilities among those over age 65 and do not at all reflect labor market discrimination against the aged.

While the probability of being counted among the *EC* poor is much lower than the probability of being counted among the *CY* poor for the preceding types, it is much higher—.21 versus .09—for the working poor. The reason is quite clear: Whereas current income depends directly on how much heads and spouses actually work, earnings capacity does not. Thus, while a strong attachment to the labor force reduces the probability of being poor in *CY* terms to a very low level, the probability of being among the *EC* poor depends upon the relative ability to generate income. Many working poor families not classified among the *CY* poor earn more than other families because they utilize their earnings capacity more fully.

Conclusions

In this chapter, we have compared and contrasted the composition of the *EC* poor with that of the *CY* poor. To the extent that our estimate of *EC* is a superior indicator of economic status, use of the *CY* measure of economic status *understates* the proportion of the poorest

11% of the total population who are black, who live in very large families, and who live in households with strong attachments to the labor market. Similarly, the *CY* measure *overstates* the proportion who live in families headed by farmers, or by persons above age 65 or below age 22, who live alone and in families with no workers. Analyzing the composition of *CY* poverty on a household basis rather than on an individual basis exacerbates these understatements and overstatements. These differences in composition between the *EC* poor and the *CY* poor hold for both the nonaged population and the total population.

In addition, we have examined the socioeconomic and demographic determinants of *EC* and *CY* poverty. It is not surprising that the effect of work status on poverty status is found to be much weaker for the *EC* measure than for the *CY*. Similarly, holding work status constant, female headship and old age per se are found to be much stronger determinants of *EC* poverty than of *CY* poverty. Finally, using the determinants regression to predict the probability that members of certain stereotypical families will be poor, we find not only that the AFDC female-headed family, the large southern rural family, and the migrant worker family have high probabilities of being poor by both measures of economic status but also that for these stereotypical families the probabilities are virtually insensitive to the measure of economic status. In contrast, the probability of being counted among the *CY* poor is much higher than the probability of being counted among the *EC* poor for the farm family, the elderly couple, and particularly the independent student. Significantly, precisely the opposite is true for the working poor family— compared to the *EC* definition, the official definition of poverty seriously understates the probability that such families will be poor.

5

Earnings Capacity and the Target Efficiency of Income Transfer Policies

We have seen that the composition of the poor population is highly dependent on the definition of economic status, and we have examined that composition using the standard current income definition and two earnings capacity definitions—$N\widetilde{E}C^*$ and $G\widetilde{E}C^*$. In this chapter, we undertake an analysis of the effectiveness with which a range of income transfer programs target their benefits on the poor. For this purpose, we define poverty by both current income and net earnings capacity ($N\widetilde{E}C^*$).

Target efficiency—the proportion of total benefits that accrues to poor families—has been used by government and academic policy analysts as a criterion for evaluating income transfer programs.[1] The emphasis on target efficiency in this chapter should not be taken to imply that this equity criterion reflects the only, or even the most important, objective by which transfer programs should be evaluated. Other criteria include the level of transfer and administrative costs, benefit "adequacy," effects on work and family structure incentives, and effects on the freedom of choice and dignity of benefi-

[1] The criterion of target efficiency was first suggested by Weisbrod (1969); see also Barth, Carcagno, and Palmer (1974).

ciaries. In this discussion, we abstract from these issues and focus only on antipoverty effectiveness. Indeed, a program's effect on some of the other objectives (such as labor supply) is not independent of its target efficiency. In analyzing the target efficiency effects, however, we will neglect this interdependence.

It should be noted that the criterion of target efficiency is useful in comparing alternative income transfer programs only if the budget available for financing each program is the same. If the budget is fixed, the proportion of it that is spent on the poor is a good measure of the program's redistributive impact, and those who attach high importance to income redistribution will prefer programs with high target efficiency. However, if the budget is not fixed—for example, if some transfer programs command greater public support than others and thereby are likely to be funded more generously—then the total benefits of the programs will differ and efficiency may not be a dependable indicator of the alternative programs' redistributive impact. Comparing social insurance programs with public assistance programs would be an example of this misleading use of the concept of target efficiency. Nor should target efficiency be taken as a measure of the *economic* efficiency—in the standard sense of resource allocation—of income transfer programs (see Garfinkel and Kesselman 1976).

In many circumstances, however, including nearly all of the alternatives analyzed here, it appears reasonable to assume that the same budget is available for alternative programs. Perhaps more important, it seems likely that the rankings of alternative programs by target efficiency are sensitive to the measure of economic status used to define the target group—the poor. This hypothesis motivates the analysis in this chapter.

Table 5.1 provides simulation estimates of the target efficiency of ten income transfer programs on both the earnings capacity ($N\widetilde{E}C^*$) and current income bases. Eight of the programs (the three negative income tax plans, the two earnings supplement plans, the two wage rate subsidy plans, and the children's allowance plan) are general proposals that are not embodied in specific legislation or administration-sponsored bills. The H.R. 1 plan for families was a Nixon administration proposal, debated at length but not passed by the Congress. Aid to Families with Dependent Children (AFDC) is an existing program. With the possible exception of the negative income tax plans, none of the proposals are intended as income support pro-

Table 5.1

TARGET EFFICIENCY OF INCOME TRANSFER PLANS ACCORDING TO EARNINGS
CAPACITY AND CURRENT INCOME DEFINITIONS OF POVERTY

	Percentage of total benefits accruing to preprogram poor		Total cost (billions of dollars)
Transfer Plan	Earnings capacity poor	Current income poor	
AFDC[a]	61	48	3.6
H.R. 1[b]	38	70	4.6
NIT$_1$[c]	45	95	4.5
NIT$_2$[c]	29	99	4.1
NIT$_3$[c]	39	65	9.7
ES$_1$[d]	37	61	3.0
ES$_2$[d]	33	50	3.6
WR$_1$[e]	22	28	6.2
WR$_2$[e]	33	44	3.3
CA[f]	16	13	4.6

[a] Aid to Families with Dependent Children program.
[b] H.R. 1—the Family Assistance Plan proposed by the Nixon Administration.
[c] Negative Income Tax Plan—see text for description of variants.
[d] Earnings Supplement Plan—see text for description of variants.
[e] Wage Rate Subsidy Plan—see text for description of variants.
[f] Children's Allowance Plan.

grams for the aged; consequently, the target efficiency and cost estimates are for the nonaged population. Poverty status based on earnings capacity is determined after the randomization process discussed in Chapter 4 and is derived from net earnings capacity.

The AFDC program provides assistance primarily to female-
headed families with children, and eligibility standards and benefit
schedules are set by state governments.[2] The simulated distribution
of the benefits and the simulated total transfer cost—$3.6 billion—of
this program are based upon recipient receipts recorded in the Current Population Survey.[3]

[2] Approximately 85% of AFDC benefits go to female-headed families. See Lurie
(1974) for a description of the benefit structure of the AFDC program.
[3] See Chapter 2, footnote 1. The Current Population Survey captures about 75% of
public assistance payments (see Projector and Bretz 1975). Our target efficiency estimates are based on the assumption that the distribution among families of unreported
benefits is the same as that of reported benefits.

H.R. 1 would have provided federal benefits of $800 per adult and $400 per child (for the first six children in a family). The first $720 of earned income would have been subject to a zero tax rate; earnings in excess of $720 per year would have been taxed at a rate of 67%. Unearned income would have been taxed at 100%. While H.R. 1 would have replaced the AFDC program, the bill contained a provision for state supplementation of basic federal benefits to minimize the adverse effect on current welfare beneficiaries. The net cost attributable to this package of policy changes is $4.6 billion.[4]

The first negative income tax plan, NIT_1, has a guarantee of $800 per adult and $400 per child (for the first six children) and a tax rate of 55% on both earned and unearned income. The second plan, NIT_2, is identical to the first except that the tax rate on unearned income is 100%. The third plan, NIT_3, is identical to the second except that the tax rate on earned income is 33% rather than 55%. In the first two plans, the breakeven level of earnings for a family of four is about $4400, while in the third plan it is $7200. While the costs of NIT_1 and NIT_2 are between $4 billion and $4.5 billion, the cost of NIT_3 is nearly $10 billion.

In an earnings supplement plan, increments to earned income are subsidized up to some stated earnings level; beyond that level, increments to earned income result in decreases in the total supplement. For earnings below the stated level, a negative tax rate (or a subsidy rate) exists; earnings above that level are subject to a benefit reduction rate similar to that of a negative income tax.[5] Estimates of the target efficiency of two variants of an earnings supplement are presented. In the first, ES_1, payments are based on *family* earned income. The supplement rate is 60% up to earnings of about $2000 (for a family of four). Increments to earnings beyond that level reduce total supplements by $.50 per dollar earned. Unearned income is subject to a zero tax rate. For a family of four, the break-even level is $4400, varying by $727 per family member for families

---

[4] The simulation program for the detailed H.R. 1 plan was designed by the Urban Institute as part of their transfer program simulation effort. See McClung, Moeller, and Siguel (1971) for a description of this program.

[5] For a discussion of the characteristics and impacts of such a program, see Haveman (1973), and Haveman, Lurie, and Mirer (1974). A variant of the earnings subsidy strategy is implicit in the earned income credit included in the Tax Reduction Act of 1975. This temporary provision has been extended in every subsequent piece of tax legislation.

larger or smaller than four.[6] The total cost of the program is $3 billion. The second earnings supplement program, ES_2, is identical to the first except that payments are based only on the head's earnings. The cost is $3.6 billion.

In a wage rate subsidy plan, income support is based on an individual's wage rate and number of hours worked. Eligible individuals with wage rates below some breakeven wage rate are entitled to a subsidy for each hour worked. Given the number of hours worked, the total benefit depends on the subsidy rate, which is a percentage of the difference between the individual's own wage rate and the breakeven wage rate of the plan. The target efficiencies of two variants of a wage rate subsidy are presented here.[7] In both plans, the breakeven wage rate is conditioned on family size. For a family of four, the breakeven wage is $2.30 per hour; incremental family members (up to eight) alter the breakeven wage by $.25 per hour per family member. The subsidy rate is 50%. In the first wage rate subsidy plan, WR_1, both family heads and spouses with wage rates below the breakeven wage rate are eligible for subsidies. In the second plan, WR_2, the subsidy depends upon the wage rate and hours worked of the family head alone. Because self-employed individuals are not likely to be eligible for wage rate subsidy programs because of severe administrative and policing problems, the target efficiency and cost estimates of WR_1 and WR_2 exclude the self-employed. These plans cost $6.2 billion and $3.3 billion, respectively.

The children's allowance plan provides a flat cash grant to families based on the number of their children. To achieve a total budgetary cost comparable to that of the other programs analyzed, we set the allowance at $60 per child.[8] The cost of the plan is $4.6 billion. This

[6] The amount of $727 was chosen to make the breakeven level of earnings for different family sizes comparable to those for NIT_1 and NIT_2. The breakeven level ceases to increase with family size at eight members.

[7] The simulation of the wage rate subsidy plan was done on the data from the Panel Study of Income Dynamics conducted by the Institute for Social Research of the University of Michigan. For a description and analyses of these data, see Morgan *et al.* (1974). Hourly wage rates are available in this data source but not in the Current Population Survey. Simulations of the NIT program on the Panel Study data yield results similar to those in the CPS; for example, the target efficiency ratios for NIT_1 and NIT_3 are 51 and 41 respectively.

[8] With the exception of NIT_3, the proposed strategies are of comparable cost magnitude. The relationship between the current income and earnings capacity target efficiencies for any one of these programs would not be significantly altered if adjustments were made to insure equal cost of programs.

proposal is the only plan analyzed for which family benefits do not vary with family income.

With the exception of AFDC and the children's allowance program, the target efficiency estimate for each program is lower when earnings capacity rather than current income is used to define poverty. This is not surprising in view of the fact that payments in the proposed programs (with the exception of the children's allowance) are based upon current income, current earnings, or current wage rates.

While 48% of the total AFDC benefits go to individuals in the bottom 9.9% of the current income distribution—the official poor—61% of total benefits go to the earnings capacity poor. Not only is AFDC more target efficient by the earnings capacity measure than by the current income measure, but the earnings capacity target efficiency of the AFDC program is much higher than that of any other program. Both of these results are attributable to the strong effect of female headship on the probability of being among the earnings capacity poor.[9]

While H.R. 1 is more target efficient than the AFDC program by the current income measure, it is much less effective in targeting its benefits on the earnings capacity poor. Only 38% of the total benefits go to the bottom 9.9% in the earnings capacity distribution. This result indicates that a significant number of people at the bottom of the current income distribution who would be aided by H.R. 1 have higher earnings capacities than individuals who would not be aided. Because our earnings capacity measure adjusts for illness and unemployment, temporary reductions in income are not likely to account for a substantial portion of this difference in ranking. Rather, these differences are attributable to differences in the preference for leisure or working in the home or particular kinds of employment with low remuneration, or to some characteristic not captured in the measurement of earnings capacity that constrains successful market activity.

The most interesting comparisons, however, can be made among the negative income tax plans, the earnings supplement plans, the wage rate subsidy plans, and the children's allowance plan. First, consider the three negative income tax plans.

[9] See the discussion in Chapter 4 of the independent effect of female headship in determining earnings capacity poverty.

The current income target efficiencies of NIT_1 and NIT_2 are close to 100%, while that of NIT_3 is only 65%. This difference is easy to explain. The breakeven level of income for a family of four in NIT_1 and NIT_2 is nearly \$4400, which is approximately the 1974 poverty line. The breakeven level in the third plan is \$7200—well above the poverty line. Thus, there is a substantial "leakage" of benefits from NIT_3 to those who are not current income poor.[10]

As with H.R. 1, the earnings capacity target efficiencies of all three NIT plans are well below the current income target efficiencies. Again, many of the official poor aided by the NIT plans have higher earnings capacities than many of those not aided—the lower current income of these families is attributable to their different taste for leisure or work in the home or occupations with low remuneration, or to some characteristic not captured in our earnings capacity measures that reduces ability to perform successfully in the labor market.

More important than this fact, however, is the similarity between the earnings capacity target efficiencies of NIT_1 and NIT_3. In direct contrast to current income target efficiency, earnings capacity target efficiency is reduced only slightly by the substantial increase in the breakeven level of income. Thus, the current income measure of poverty is misleading in implying that NIT programs with low breakeven levels of income are more target efficient than NIT programs with higher breakeven levels. While there may be reasons, such as costs or possible work disincentive effects, for preferring NIT proposals with low breakeven levels, our estimates indicate that—if earnings capacity is preferred to current income as an indicator of economic status—the difference in target efficiency is not one of them.

The least target efficient NIT program (in terms of earnings capacity) is NIT_2—the program with a tax rate on unearned income of 100%. In view of the fact that female heads of household both receive a large proportion of the unearned income that accrues to the nonaged low-income population and are extremely likely to be among

---

[10] The breakeven level of income is far and away the most important parameter of a program in determining target efficiency when poverty is defined by current income. We simulated an additional NIT plan with a \$7200 breakeven level of income which had a higher guarantee (\$1200 per adult, \$600 per child) and tax rate (50%) than those in NIT_3. But its current income target efficiency estimate was virtually identical to that for NIT_3, 66% as opposed to 65%.

the earnings capacity poor, this result is not surprising. Programs with 100% tax rates on unearned income will provide much smaller benefits to the AFDC population than programs with lower tax rates and therefore will provide a smaller proportion of their total benefits to the earnings capacity poor. That earnings capacity target efficiency turns out to be more sensitive to the tax rate on unearned income than to the breakeven level of earnings is an unexpected result, however.

Next, examine the target efficiency estimates of the earnings supplement and wage rate subsidy plans. As before, the estimates are substantially lower when target efficiency measures are based on earnings capacity rather than current income. Of particular interest, however, is the comparison of these estimates to those for the NIT programs. When poverty is measured by current income, the target efficiency measures of the earnings supplement and wage rate subsidy programs are well below those for the NIT programs. However, when poverty is measured by earnings capacity, the differences are smaller. For the earnings supplement plans, the target efficiency estimates based on earnings capacity range from 33% to 37%, as compared to the 29% to 45% range of the negative income tax plans. Similarly, the earnings capacity target efficiency of the wage rate subsidy confined to family heads (WR_2) is relatively close to that of the negative income tax plans. Only the wage rate subsidy based on both head and spouse earnings (WR_1) is less target efficient in terms of earnings capacity than any of the NIT programs. Benefits from this plan accrue to many families in which the wife earns a low wage while the family head commands a relatively high wage. Again, if earnings capacity is more accurate than current income as an indicator of economic status, target efficiency is not a reason for preferring a negative income tax over an earnings supplement or a wage rate subsidy to family heads.

Finally, consider the children's allowance. As noted earlier, if the budget for a program such as a children's allowance (which is not income tested) is larger than the budget for an income-tested program, then a comparison based on the assumption that the program budgets are the same size will underestimate the redistribution potential of the non-income-tested program relative to the income-tested program. Even so, it is useful to compare the target efficiencies of the income-tested programs to that of the children's allowance program under the current income and earnings capacity definitions of poverty.

Since the children's allowance benefits are paid to all families with children, irrespective of income, it is not surprising that the current income target efficiency of the children's allowance program is lower than that of any of the income-tested programs. Yet under the earnings capacity definition of poverty, the difference between the target efficiency of the children's allowance program and that of the NIT, ES, and WR programs is much less dramatic. Whereas the NIT plan with a low breakeven level is between seven and eight times more target efficient than the children's allowance by the current income definition of poverty, it is only between two and three times as target efficient (depending on the tax rate on unearned income) by the earnings capacity definition. Indeed, the absolute difference in earnings capacity target efficiency is larger between NIT_1 and NIT_2 than between NIT_1 and the children's allowance program. Thus when economic status is measured by earnings capacity rather than current income, even children's allowance programs do not appear to be markedly inferior to NIT programs in terms of target efficiency.

Two major conclusions emerge from this chapter's examination of the degree to which 10 different transfer programs target their benefits on the current income and earnings capacity nonaged poor. First, estimates of target efficiency are very sensitive to the definition of poverty. With the exception of the AFDC and children's allowance programs, the earnings capacity target efficiency of each program is lower—in many cases much lower—than the current income target efficiency. Second, and more important, the impression that NIT programs with low breakeven levels of income are far more target efficient than the other transfer programs disappears when earnings capacity replaces current income as the measure of economic status.

6

Labor Market Discrimination and Black–White Differences in Economic Status

A serious disparity between blacks and whites in both earnings and incomes has persisted during the period since World War II. The ratio of black to white median total family income has increased from about .50 shortly after the war to .62 in 1975 (U.S. Bureau of the Census 1971). Numerous studies have been undertaken both to track changes in this differential over time and to ascertain the factors that account for its persistence.[1]

The empirical results presented in this chapter are in the tradition of these previous studies. The objective is, first, to discern the extent of black–white differentials in economic status for a recent period. Racial differences in income, earnings, and earnings capacity in 1973 are presented for both the total and nonaged populations and for both individuals and families. Second, the relative contribution of labor market discrimination to the earnings differential is estimated. The following questions are addressed: If labor market discrimination were eliminated, by how much would the black–white dif-

[1] See, for example, Batchelder (1964); Ashenfelter (1970); Gwartney (1970); Wohlstetter and Coleman (1970); Blinder (1973); Christensen and Bernard (1974); Kiker and Liles (1974); and Vroman (1974).

70

ferential in earnings be reduced? Does the severity of labor market discrimination vary with earnings capacity? How much would inequality in the United States be reduced if labor market discrimination against blacks were eliminated? Finally, as has not been done in any other study, we explicitly examine the reliability of the methodology used to estimate the contribution of labor market discrimination to racial differences in earnings.

The data base employed is the Panel Study of Income Dynamics conducted by the University of Michigan's Institute for Social Research.[2] The specification of the earnings functions used for deriving the earnings capacity estimates is similar to that described in Chapter 3. However, instead of the broad measures of work effort available in the CPS (full time versus part time and number of weeks worked last year), we used a measure of annual hours worked per year (constructed from number of weeks worked times average hours worked per week). Moreover, in addition to the standard human capital and demographic variables used in the CPS earnings functions, variables measuring verbal ability, achievement orientation, public school expenditures per pupil, parents' income, and father's education were employed. These earnings functions are presented in Appendix D.

Racial Differences in Economic Status

Differences in economic status between blacks and whites within the total population are illustrated in Table 6.1, where the black–white ratios of pretransfer income (PTY),[3] earnings (E), gross earnings capacity (GEC), and net earnings capacity (NEC) are presented for families in the total and nonaged populations.[4] For men and women, only the ratios of E and EC are presented. In addition to the mean ratios of these measures, the table contains the ratios at the

[2] See Morgan et al. (1974) for a description of these data and analyses of them.

[3] Because of our ultimate focus on the role of labor market discrimination and differences in human capital, we deal here with pretransfer rather than total family income. In focusing on comparisons over the entire distribution, our analysis follows that of Wohlstetter and Coleman (1970) who emphasized the inadequacy of estimates at only the median of the distributions.

[4] These ratios are calculated for the head and spouse in a family and hence neglect the earnings and earnings capacity of workers in addition to the head and spouse.

Table 6.1

BLACK–WHITE RATIOS OF INCOME, EARNINGS, AND EARNINGS CAPACITY:
TOTAL AND NONAGED POPULATIONS

	Mean	Percentile of distribution curve				
		10	25	50	75	90
Total families						
E	.58	—	.15	.47	.62	.67
PTY	.54	—	.11	.44	.59	.66
GEC	.58	.48	.52	.52	.61	.65
NEC	.52	.24	.39	.48	.59	.63
Men						
E	.63	—	.44	.65	.67	.71
EC	.67	.56	.63	.69	.69	.69
Women						
E	.90	—	—	2.80	.86	.87
EC	.74	.61	.67	.75	.77	.79
Nonaged families						
E	.56	—	.20	.48	.60	.68
PTY	.53	—	.19	.45	.59	.65
GEC	.58	.51	.47	.52	.62	.64
NEC	.52	.19	.39	.49	.59	.63
Men						
E	.66	.21	.64	.67	.69	.70
EC	.68	.64	.67	.68	.69	.67
Women						
E	.87	—	—	1.15	.89	.84
EC	.75	.65	.69	.76	.77	.79

tenth, twenty-fifth, fiftieth, seventy-fifth, and ninetieth percentiles of
the black and white earnings capacity distributions.

Several points are worth noting. First, Table 6.1 indicates that in
1973 mean family earnings of blacks were 58% of those of whites; at
the median, the black–white earnings ratio is only .47 for both
groups. For the nonaged population, the earnings ratio at the mean is
even lower—.56. These family ratios are lower than those for either
men or women. At the mean, the black–white earnings ratio for men
is .63, and that for women is .90. This discrepancy is attributable to
the high percentage of spouses in two-parent white families with zero
or very low earnings. Moreover, the black–white disparity in earnings

capacity is also greater for families than for men only. Thus comparisons that focus on racial differences in men's earnings understate the racial differences in family well-being.

Second, for both the total and nonaged populations, the net earnings capacity ratios (*NEC*) are smaller than the earnings or income ratios. This suggests that the commonly stated black–white differences understate the actual disparity between the races in economic well-being.

Third, the black–white *NEC* ratios (and with one minor exception the black–white *GEC* ratios) in both the total and the nonaged populations increase monotonically over the entire distribution of earnings capacity, suggesting that racial differences in earnings capacity are more serious at the bottom than at the top of the distribution.

Fourth, the *GEC* ratios tend to be larger than the *NEC* ratios— and, for nonaged families, larger than the earnings ratios. *NEC* adjusts for child care while *GEC* does not. On average, blacks have larger families than whites, and the racial differences in family size are more pronounced at the bottom of the *NEC* distribution than at the top. This accounts for the low *NEC* ratios at the bottom of the distribution.

Fifth, the ratios are generally larger for families in the total population than those in the nonaged population. This indicates that black aged people earn more relative to white aged people than do black nonaged relative to white nonaged. The longer average life of whites is likely to be the main cause of this result.

Finally, for men—both total and nonaged—the mean *EC* ratio is higher than the mean *E* ratio while the opposite is true for women. This reflects the fact that black women utilize a higher proportion of their earnings capacity than do white women, as Chapter 5 indicates.

In a rough way, these results can be compared with estimates for 1967 developed by Wohlstetter and Coleman (1970). The pattern they found for families over the income distribution is similar to the one we find over the *NEC* distribution: The ratio at the median income lies above that at lower levels of the distribution and below that at higher levels of the distribution.[5] Similarly, both sets of

[5] The comparison of absolute ratios at various points in the distribution is not possible because Wohlstetter and Coleman used total family income while we employ pretransfer income. At the median for families, Wohlstetter and Coleman found a ratio of .62, compared to our ratios of .44 (total population) and .45 (nonaged population). Because black families receive higher transfers on average than white families, Wohlstetter and Coleman's ratio is consistent with ours.

results indicate that this disparity over the nonaged distribution is less extreme for men only than it is for families.[6]

The Role of Labor Market Discrimination

In this section, we attempt to separate the role of economic discrimination in labor markets from the roles of other variables that contribute to the gap between black and white earnings and income. The contribution of labor market discrimination to the black–white income gap is relevant in formulating policies designed to eliminate or at least reduce the gap. If a substantial portion of the gap is attributable to labor market discrimination, then, ceteris paribus, a substantial portion of the total resources devoted to reducing the gap should be spent on eliminating labor market discrimination.[7] We also seek to discover whether the severity of labor market discrimination varies with earnings capacity. John Kenneth Galbraith, for example, has asserted that labor market discrimination is now most severe against blacks of high capacity (see Galbraith, Kuh, and Thurow 1971). First, we present a conceptual framework for analyzing the components of the racial earnings gap; then we summarize our findings on the role of labor market discrimination.

Conceptual Framework and
Empirical Problems

Observed differentials between black and white income and earnings have been attributed to numerous factors, some of which are manifestations of present or past discrimination against blacks. For

[6] Comparing our results for men in the nonaged population with those of Wohlstetter and Coleman (p. 45) yields similar conclusions. Throughout the distribution, however, our earnings ratios lie about .10 above those of Wohlstetter and Coleman, indicating some improvement in the relative status of black men between 1967 and 1973.

[7] Whether or not a greater share of resources should be devoted to combating labor market discrimination depends upon the marginal benefits and costs of this and alternative expenditures. As Masters (1975, p. 152) has pointed out, however, the proportion of total resources devoted to reducing racial earnings differentials that goes to combating labor market discrimination is so small relative to the proportion of the earnings gap accounted for by labor market discrimination that it is hard to believe that the current mix is optimal.

example, of the current adult population, blacks were provided not only with less education but also with education of a lower quality than whites. Thus, other things being equal, blacks of prime working age have less human capital than whites, and one would expect black earnings to be lower than white earnings. Black earnings will also fall below white earnings if blacks with certain characteristics are paid lower wages than whites with the same characteristics. While the former case illustrates the role of past discrimination in education, the latter case illustrates the impact of current labor market discrimination.

Other factors, possibly unrelated to racial discrimination, may contribute to the racial income differential. Relative to whites, for example, blacks may have a stronger preference for leisure over income and choose to work fewer weeks per year or hours per week. Another possibility is that, on average, blacks may have a stronger aversion to school attendance than do whites, voluntarily choosing less education and lower earnings capacity. Finally, the black and white populations may have different demographic structures: A smaller proportion of blacks may be at the peak earnings level of the life cycle.

While the number of possible contributing factors to observed black–white income differences is very large, the vast bulk of them can be subsumed in the following four categories:

1. *Differences in human capital endowments.* For a number of reasons, the black population may have a smaller stock of human capital than the white population. As suggested earlier, past discrimination in the provision of public education may explain a part of this disparity. Another possible reason is that blacks may tend to come from regions with relatively weak tastes for education compared to other private or public consumption, or from relatively poor regions that could not afford high expenditures on education. Related to this last point, black adults, compared to white adults, may have grown up in homes in which parents placed relatively slight emphasis on or could afford relatively little expenditure for schooling and human investment. Finally, some have suggested that blacks simply have less innate ability than whites.

2. *Differences in demographic structure.* A part of the difference in black–white incomes may be caused by demographic factors, such as differences in the age structures of blacks and whites. Similarly,

blacks may reside in regions in which the wage structure is relatively low. While this factor might correct itself in the long run, in any given year it may contribute to observed income differences, and the greater proportion of female-headed households or of larger families among blacks may also contribute to the observed differential.

3. *Voluntary differences in work effort or capacity utilization.* Perhaps blacks simply choose to work fewer hours in a year than whites. This factor might be manifested in a greater aversion to job search, a greater preference for unemployment or nonparticipation in the labor force, or a preference for occupations in which part-time, part-year jobs are heavily represented or in which the norm of hours worked is relatively low.

4. *Labor market discrimination.* A final factor contributing to black–white income differences may be differences in the ways employers respond to the skills and abilities of blacks and whites. For two individuals with the same skills and abilities, one black and one white, employers may offer a lower wage rate or fewer hours of work to the black, give preference to the white in allocating overtime hours, or simply hire the white before the black.

If data on individual attributes and tastes were complete and if a statistical model incorporating these variables and their relationships could be correctly specified, the contributions of each factor to observed income differentials could be discerned. Presuming for a moment that such an ideal situation did exist, the following two-stage statistical procedure could be employed. First, completely specified earnings functions would be fitted for both blacks and whites. These functions would be of the following form:

$$E_B = a_1 + a_2 \mathbf{HC}_B + a_3 \mathbf{T}_B + a_4 \mathbf{D}_B$$
$$E_W = b_1 + b_2 \mathbf{HC}_W + b_3 \mathbf{T}_W + b_4 \mathbf{D}_W,$$

where E_B and E_W represent the earnings of individual blacks and whites, $\mathbf{HC}_B$ and $\mathbf{HC}_W$ represent vectors of human capital characteristics of blacks and whites, $\mathbf{T}_B$ and $\mathbf{T}_W$ represent vectors of taste characteristics of blacks and whites, and $\mathbf{D}_B$ and $\mathbf{D}_W$ represent vectors of demographic characteristics of blacks and whites. If these two functions were accurately specified and all relevant human capital, taste, and demographic variables were included, the r^2 would be unity for each equation and the vectors of regression coefficients

$(a_2, a_3,$ and a_4 and $b_2, b_3,$ and $b_4)$ would capture the effects on black and white earnings of human capital, taste, and demographic factors respectively. Then, having fitted both of these equations and having obtained the structure by which both blacks and whites transform their characteristics into earnings, we could use the *black* HC, T, and D variables in the *white* equation with the white regression coefficients. From this procedure, we could estimate the earnings blacks would receive *if* the labor market treated them the same as whites of identical HC, T, and D characteristics. The difference between these projected black earnings and actual white earnings would be attributable to difference in HC, T, and D. The difference between the projected black earnings and actual black earnings would be the result of labor market discrimination.[8]

Unfortunately, implementation of this ideal procedure presents many difficulties. Available data allow only incomplete identification of the vectors of HC, T, and D characteristics for either blacks or whites. If unobserved HC, T, or D exist and if these unobserved variables favor whites over blacks, the difference between black earnings and white earnings estimated using the white equation will be biased downward. Treating labor market discrimination as a residual, as the above procedure implies, would then lead to an upward bias in the estimate of the role of labor market discrimination in determining income differentials.

On the other hand, it is possible that the inclusion of some variables for which data are available may lead to a downward bias in the estimate of the importance of labor market discrimination. For example, if verbal ability depends upon what kind of a job an individual has, and if the kinds of jobs black and white individuals get are affected by labor market discrimination, treating labor market discrimination as a residual after controlling for verbal ability will lead to an underestimate of labor market discrimination.[9]

---

[8] The white earnings function reflects the benefits that whites derive from labor market discrimination against blacks. Thus, if labor market discrimination were eliminated, black characteristics would not be rewarded quite as generously as identical white characteristics currently are rewarded. But since there are so many more whites than blacks, the effect on the white earnings function of eliminating labor market discrimination should be very small—especially compared to the effect on the black earnings function. Consequently inserting black characteristics into the white earnings function was the procedure chosen.

[9] For example, it is likely that, ceteris paribus, the verbal ability scores of individuals with white-collar jobs will be higher than those of individuals with blue-collar

In general, there are problems associated with classifying variables for which data are available. Because the effort here is to distinguish the role of labor market discrimination from that of other factors, the most serious categorization difficulties have to do with variables concerned with the quantity of work. Should the fact that black men work fewer hours per year (or experience more unemployment, or have a lower rate of labor force participation, or work less overtime) than white men be attributed to differences in tastes for income relative to leisure, or to labor market discrimination? The estimated importance of labor market discrimination is likely to vary widely, depending on how these differences are categorized.

Empirical Procedure and Assumptions

The empirical procedure adopted in this analysis follows the four-part categorization of the previous section and employs the two-stage methodology for estimating labor market discrimination's role in determining black–white income differences. First, earnings functions are fitted for black and white men and women. Given the superior data available in the OEO Michigan Survey, these functions minimize the domain of unmeasured characteristics that affect individual earnings. Nevertheless, some potentially relevant variables, such as physical features, are not included at all; while for others, such as IQ and education provided in the home, we have only proxy variables—verbal ability, parental income, and father's education. We will assume that the remaining unmeasured characteristics are uncorrelated with race and other independent variables.

Even if all differences in human capital between blacks and whites were perfectly measured, it would still be necessary to make some assumptions about racial differences in tastes for leisure relative to income in order to ascertain how much of the black–white earnings differential is attributable to labor market discrimination. Holding human capital and demographic characteristics constant, black men work fewer hours than white men, while black women work more

---

jobs. Similarly, if blacks complete fewer years of schooling than whites because labor market discrimination makes the rate of return to schooling lower for blacks than for whites, the role of past labor market discrimination in accounting for the present earnings gap and the role of current labor market discrimination in accounting for the earnings gap of the next generation of adults will be underestimated.

hours than white women. Black men are unemployed more weeks per year than white men. A larger proportion of black men are not labor force participants; a larger proportion work only part time during the weeks they work; and a smaller proportion work more than the standard 40-hour week. These differences in work effort may be caused by differences in the demand for black labor vis-à-vis white labor resulting from labor market discrimination, differences between blacks and whites in taste for income versus leisure, or some combination of both. Previous studies have not treated this taste variable consistently; some have implicitly assumed that taste differences between blacks and whites do not account for differences in hours worked per year, while others have assumed the opposite. We develop estimates of the role of labor market discrimination under both assumptions. Our lower bound estimate assumes that all such work effort differences are attributable to racial differences in tastes; our upper bound estimate attributes all racial differences in work effort to labor market discrimination.

Finally, while we assume that differences between the hourly wage rates of blacks and whites with identical human capital and demographic characteristics are attributable to discrimination alone, even though one could argue that part of these differences results from different tastes. The case would hinge on the concept of compensating variations in wage rates—higher wage rates to compensate for undesirable nonpecuniary aspects of a job, lower wage rates to compensate for desirable nonpecuniary aspects of a job. However, the nonpecuniary aspects of the jobs held by blacks are generally conceded to be less desirable than those of jobs held by whites with similar human capital characteristics. We therefore assume that all differences between the hourly wage rates of blacks and those of whites with identical human capital and demographic characteristics are attributable to labor market discrimination.

Measuring the Effect of Labor Market Discrimination

In this section, we seek to isolate empirically the part of the total earnings gap that is attributable to labor market discrimination. The earnings gap, G, is defined as

$$G = E_W - E_B \qquad (6.1)$$

and is calculated by subtracting the total earnings of all white units divided by the number of white units from the total earnings of all black units divided by the number of black units. Other aggregate gaps are calculated similarly.

As a first step in the analysis, we calculate a lower bound estimate of the effect of labor market discrimination. Accordingly, we assume that all differences in hours worked—both within and between races—except those attributable to health status, are attributable to voluntary choice. These differences can be eliminated from the earnings gap by substituting for G an estimate of what both black and white individuals would earn if they both worked the same number of hours—in effect, an estimate of earnings capacity of the individuals in both groups. To obtain a lower bound estimate, we used the annual hours worked by blacks as the norm.[10] Given these assumptions, the amount of G attributable to factors other than differences in tastes can be designated as

$$G_T^L = EC_W(H_B) - EC_B(H_B), \qquad (6.2)$$

where $EC_W(H_B)$ is the amount that any white would earn if he worked the annual hours of a black with comparable earnings capacity and $EC_B(H_B)$ is the predicted earnings of each black, given his human capital, demographic characteristics and actual hours worked.

With differences in work effort eliminated as factors in determining black–white earnings differentials, the remaining gap (G_T^L) is attributable to human capital, demographic characteristics, and labor market discrimination. As the next step, the contribution to earnings differentials of racial differences in human capital and demographic characteristics can be estimated. This is done by employing the white earnings functions to estimate the earnings capacity of both blacks and whites. To estimate the earnings capacity of blacks, the black values of the independent variables are used with the white regression coefficients. The effect of this is to simulate the earnings blacks would have if the labor market responded to black human capital and demographic characteristics

---

[10] Note that the estimate of labor market discrimination will be sensitive to the choice of hours worked as a norm. If we had used either the hours of whites or 2000 hours rather than the hours of blacks, the labor market discrimination estimate would be increased. In this sense, the choice of black hours worked as the norm is consistent with the object of obtaining a lower bound estimate of labor market discrimination.

as it does to white. From this procedure, the contribution of differences in human capital and demographic characteristics to black–white earnings differences (G_{HCD}^L) can be designated as

$$G_{HCD}^L = EC_W(H_B) - EC_B^W(H_B), \qquad (6.3)$$

in which $EC_B^W(H_B)$ is the amount an individual black would earn at his actual hours worked if his human capital and demographic characteristics were rewarded as those of whites in the market place. (Note that this simulation procedure does not increase the earnings of blacks who do not work.) G_{HCD}^L, then, is interpreted as the portion of the full earnings gap (G) accounted for by differences between blacks and whites in human capital and demographic characteristics.

We can now estimate as a residual the portion of the total earnings gap that is attributable to labor market discrimination. It is the difference between G_T and G_{HCD}, or

$$G_{LMD}^L = G_T^L - G_{HCD}^L = [EC_W(H_B) - EC_B(H_B)] - [EC_W(H_B)$$
$$- EC_B^W(H_B)] \qquad (6.4)$$
$$= EC_B^W(H_B) - EC_B(H_B).$$

In short, our lower bound estimate of labor market discrimination is equal to what each black would earn at his actual hours worked if his human capital and demographic characteristics were rewarded in the market place as those of whites minus what he actually earns. These differences are summed over all blacks who worked and then divided by the number of blacks who work.

An upper bound estimate of the portion of the total earnings gap accounted for by labor market discrimination can be obtained by assuming that none of the difference between blacks and whites in hours worked is due to voluntary choice. Implicit in this procedure is the assumption that all differences between blacks and whites in hours worked are due to labor market discrimination; that it is only because of employer discrimination that blacks are unemployed more than whites, work part time more than whites, work overtime less than whites, and are out of the labor force more than whites. As a first step in obtaining this upper bound estimate, therefore, we substitute $EC_W(H_W)$ for E_W and $EC_B(H_B)$ for E_B, and rewrite G:

$$G = E_W - E_B = EC_W(H_W) - EC_B(H_B). \qquad (6.5)$$

From this gap, we now remove the effect of differences between blacks and whites in human capital and demographic characteristics. This is done by employing the white earnings functions to estimate the earnings capacity of both blacks and whites. To obtain the upper bound estimate, we assume that in the absence of discrimination blacks would work as much as whites. Hence, we employ the hours worked of whites with comparable earnings capacities to blacks, H_W^*, in estimating the contribution of human capital and demographic characteristics to black–white earnings differences.[11] The upper bound measure of the proportion of the racial earnings gap attributable to labor market discrimination is then equal to

$$G_{LMD}^U = G - G_{HCD}^U = [EC_W(H_W) - EC_B(H_B)] - [EC_W(H_W)$$
$$- EC_B^W(H_W^*)] \qquad (6.6)$$
$$= EC_B^W(H_W^*) - EC_B(H_B).$$

In Appendix E the upper and lower bound measures of the contribution of labor market discrimination to racial earnings differentials are stated formally.

For women, the upper bound estimate lacks a clear interpretation. Because black women work more than white women, the upper bound estimate for women is actually lower than the lower bound estimate. Consequently upper bound estimates for women are not presented. Upper bound estimates for families, however, are presented. Implicit in these estimates is the assumption that black women work more than white women as a response to discrimination against black men and that if such discrimination were eliminated black women would work the same amount as white women. To the

---

[11] An estimate of the hours worked by a white with earnings capacity equivalent to each black observation was estimated as follows: (a) the earnings capacity at 2000 hours for each white was calculated—$EC_W(2000)$; (b) the hours worked of whites was regressed against the measure of earnings capacity; (c) the earnings capacity of each black (evaluated at 2000 hours) assuming his characteristics were rewarded as are those of whites was calculated by substituting the black's characteristics into the white earnings regressions—$EC_B^W(2000)$, and (d) this estimate [$EC_B^W(2000)$] of black earnings capacity in the absence of labor market discrimination was employed in the regression of hours worked on earnings capacity for whites to ascertain how many hours a white with comparable earnings capacity to the black in question would work. The term $EC_B^W(H_W)$ was then reevaluated using this estimate of H_W^*, and designated as $EC_B^W(H_W^*)$.

extent that black women are discriminated against in hours as well as wage rates, our upper bound estimates for families will be an underestimate.

Estimates of Labor Market Discrimination

In Table 6.2 we present the following empirical results: the average earnings gap; mean black earnings; lower and upper bound estimates of the average cost of labor market discrimination to black men, black women, and black families; lower and upper bound estimates of the proportion of the earnings gap (G) that is attributable to labor market discrimination; and lower and upper bound estimates of the percentage increase in black earnings that would result from the elimination of labor market discrimination.

Several points are worth noting. First, the estimates of labor market discrimination as a percentage of the earnings gap for men

Table 6.2

LABOR MARKET DISCRIMINATION (*LMD*) AND THE RACIAL
EARNINGS GAP: NONAGED POPULATION

	Men	Women	Families
Mean earnings gap	3670	349	4499
Mean black earnings	6352	2175	5808
Mean dollar value of *LMD*			
Lower bound estimate	1574	416	1332
Upper bound estimate	2209		1735
Mean dollar value of *LMD* as a proportion of mean earnings gap			
Lower bound estimate	.43	>100%	.30
Upper bound estimate	.60		.39
Mean dollar value of *LMD* as a proportion of mean black earnings			
Lower bound estimate	.25	.19	.23
Upper bound estimate	.35		.30

NOTE: Except where noted, all values are expressed in dollars.

are sensitive to assumptions about the source of racial differences in hours worked. When differences in taste are assumed to account for the differences in hours worked, the estimated cost to black males of labor market discrimination is $1574; when labor market discrimination is assumed to account for the differences in hours worked, the estimated cost of labor market discrimination is $2209. Similarly, depending upon the assumption regarding the source of racial differences in hours worked, the proportion of the gap attributable to labor market discrimination varies from .43 to .60.

The lower bound estimates of the proportion of the total earnings gap accounted for by labor market discrimination are comparable to estimates by other researchers (see especially Gwartney 1970; Blinder 1973; Masters 1974) and suggest that the elimination of labor market discrimination would increase black men's earnings by 25% and remove 43% of the earnings gap between blacks and whites. These figures rise to 35% and 60%, respectively, if the upper bound estimates are used.

Labor market discrimination against women appears to be somewhat less severe in absolute terms. We estimate that if labor market discrimination were eliminated the earnings of black women would increase by 19%. Because black women work more than white women—thus reducing the gap in earnings—the proportion of the total earnings gap between black women and white women accounted for by labor market discrimination is greater than 100%.

The effect of labor market discrimination on family earnings is intermediate to its effect on men's and women's earnings. This condition exists because such a large proportion (33%) of black families are headed by women. Thus our estimates suggest that if labor market discrimination were eliminated, the earnings of black families would increase by between 23% and 30%. Similarly, between 30% and 39% of the total gap in earnings between black and white families is attributable to labor market discrimination.

Reliability of the Methodology

One major shortcoming of the methodology we use to obtain estimates of labor market discrimination is that omitted variables that are correlated with both race and earnings will lead to biases in the estimates. It is, of course, impossible to determine precisely the seriousness of this problem, but the reliability of this residual-type methodology can be tested by using the same methodology to predict the amount of labor market discrimination against a group that earns substantially less than the dominant group but is not commonly believed to be discriminated against.[12]

Just as there are differences in earnings and human capital between whites and blacks, there are also differences in earnings and human capital between southern-born whites and other whites. Southern-born white men earn about $2000 per year less, have 1.5 fewer years of schooling, and score .6 points lower (on a 13-point scale) on the verbal ability test given as part of the Michigan Income Dynamics Panel Study than other white men. But whereas strong evidence exists that there is substantial labor market discrimination against blacks, no such evidence exists that there is substantial labor market discrimination against southern-born whites. Any discrimination against southern-born whites would have to be on the basis of accent. Yet 85% of our sample of southern-born whites still reside in the South. Consequently, even if there is some labor market discrimination against men with southern accents, the effect of such labor market discrimination on the average earnings of all southern-born white men should be very small.

If the estimate of labor market discrimination against southern-born whites derived from the residual methodology is close to zero, confidence in the residual methodology will be enhanced. If the esti-

---

[12] This kind of test was suggested to us by Morgan O. Reynolds and William W. Brown. In an unpublished manuscript entitled "Discrimination and the Residual Approach," they show that, holding constant years of schooling, scholastic achievement, sex, and race, individuals who reside in the South earn less than those who reside in the North. They argue that it is neither more nor less reasonable to attribute this difference to labor market discrimination than it is to attribute the comparable difference in black–white earnings to labor market discrimination. We disagree, for two reasons. First, a more appropriate test—which we describe in the text—is to compare whites born in the South to other whites while holding current residence constant. Both living standards and costs of living are lower in the South than elsewhere. Second, there is a substantial amount of empirical documentation of the existence of labor market discrimination based on race. During the 1970s, for example, over 16,000 charges of racial discrimination were filed annually with the Equal Employment Opportunity Commission (EEOC). Of the 1729 cases filed in 1969 in which the EEOC made determinations by 1972 (most cases are settled short of determination), in 800 cases, or nearly half, the EEOC found that there was discrimination (see Beller 1974, p. 252).

mate of labor market discrimination is significantly greater than zero, confidence in the residual methodology will be reduced. It is possible, of course, that other omitted variables exist that are correlated with race but not with region of birth. For this reason, our findings are only suggestive.

Not surprisingly, our results suggest that our amount of confidence in the residual methodology depends on the comprehensiveness of the model. When we include in our regression equations only the variables of years of schooling, age, current region, and city size, our lower bound estimate of labor market discrimination against southern-born whites is $600. (The comparable estimate for discrimination against blacks is $1644.) When we use more comprehensive earnings functions, including variables for verbal ability, father's education and income, and per pupil school expenditures, the estimate of labor market discrimination against southern-born whites is actually negative.[13] Although these findings do not demonstrate that the residual methodology yields unbiased estimates of labor market discrimination against blacks, they do enhance our confidence in the methodology.

Labor Market Discrimination and the
Distribution of Earnings Capacity

In this section we seek to determine if the severity of labor market discrimination varies systematically over the distribution of black earnings capacity. The measure of the severity of labor market discrimination used is the ratio of earnings foregone because of labor market discrimination in a quintile to mean black earnings in that quintile. As before, lower and upper bound estimates of labor market

[13] Although the estimate is about $300, this is probably not statistically significant. A test of the statistical significance of the labor market discrimination estimates is quite difficult to make. Two standard errors must enter the calculation: First, there is the standard error associated with the estimate of what blacks would earn if they were treated like whites. This standard error is derived from the white equation. Second, there is the standard error associated with the estimate of what blacks actually earn. The assumptions required to combine these two estimates are strong.

discrimination are presented. The lower and upper bound estimates (LMD_L and LMD_U) in each quintile are

$$LMD_L = EC^W_{BQ}(H^B_{BQ}) - EC^B_{BQ}(H^B_{BQ}) \qquad (6.7)$$

$$LMD_U = EC^W_{BQ}(H^W_{BQ}) - EC^B_{BQ}(H^B_{BQ}). \qquad (6.8)$$

The first term in the lower bound estimate indicates what blacks in quintile Q would earn if they were rewarded in the market as whites with the same characteristics are rewarded and if both groups worked the same hours as blacks in quintile Q. (Note that blacks in quintile Q are being compared to whites with identical characteristics not to whites in quintile Q in the white distribution. The latter comparison is presented in the first section of this chapter.) The second term indicates what blacks in quintile Q actually earn. Similarly, the first term in the upper bound estimate indicates the amount blacks in quintile Q would earn if their characteristics were rewarded as white characteristics are and if they worked the same number of hours as whites with the same characteristics.

In Table 6.3 we present our estimates of labor market discrimination by quintile for both men and women. Estimates of the absolute dollar value of discrimination and of discrimination as a proportion of mean black earnings in the quintile are presented.

Table 6.3

LABOR MARKET DISCRIMINATION (*LMD*) AS A FUNCTION OF EARNINGS CAPACITY

	Quintile in earnings capacity distribution				
	1	2	3	4	5
Men					
LMD_L	1244	1502	1577	1583	1855
LMD_U	1265	1805	2054	3015	2842
LMD_L/E^Q_{BQ}	.36	.31	.25	.22	.19
LMD_U/E^Q_{BQ}	.36	.37	.33	.42	.29
Women					
LMD_L	513	348	463	489	320
LMD_L/E_{BQ}	.45	.24	.23	.20	.08

Measured in absolute terms, the data for men tend to confirm Galbraith's hypothesis that discrimination against high-capacity blacks is more severe than against low-capacity blacks. The lower bound estimates increase monotonically from the first to the fourth quintile, the fifth quintile being somewhat lower than the fourth. But it may be more appropriate to measure the severity of labor market discrimination in a quintile as a percentage of the earnings of blacks in that quintile. The lower bound estimates in the second panel of the table indicate that the percentage increase in black earnings if labor market discrimination were eliminated is inversely related to earnings capacity. Measured in percentage terms, the labor market discrimination is nearly twice as large in the bottom quintile as it is in the top quintile—36% as opposed to 19%. The upper bound estimates indicate that severity of labor market discrimination is not systematically related to earnings capacity. The largest percentage increase (42%) would be experienced by blacks in the fourth quintile, while the smallest increase would be experienced by those in the fifth. Thus if the severity of labor market discrimination is more appropriately measured in percentage terms, the evidence does not support Galbraith's assertion.

In absolute terms, the amount of discrimination against black women is not systematically related to earnings capacity. The relatively flat pattern in the absolute measure implies that as a percentage of black earnings, labor market discrimination is inversely related to earnings capacity. Thus, the elimination of labor market discrimination would lead to an increase of 45% in the earnings of black women in the first quintile but an increase of only 8% in the fifth.

In summary, our results provide little basis for focusing policies designed to combat labor market discrimination on one part of the distribution of earnings capacity. Rather, the results suggest that at least for men, labor market discrimination is serious across the entire distribution of earnings capacity.

Labor Market Discrimination and Inequality

In this section, we estimate how much less inequality there would be in the United States if there were no labor market discrimination.

Table 6.4

THE EFFECT OF RACIAL LABOR MARKET DISCRIMINATION ON
INEQUALITY

	Actual Gini	Gini after simulating end of *LMD*
Total family income	.479	.451
Pretransfer family income	.540	.526

The methodology is similar to that employed in the last two sections: We first obtain upper and lower bound estimates of how much more each black in the sample would earn if his characteristics were rewarded like white characteristics in the market. We then add these estimates to actual earnings to obtain lower and upper bound estimates of what blacks would earn in the absence of discrimination. Finally, we recompute Gini coefficients for the nonaged population using the adjusted earnings figures for black families.

In Table 6.4, we present Gini coefficients for pretransfer and total family income using both actual and adjusted earnings figures for black families. The coefficients are similar. Labor market discrimination does not account for a significant portion of total inequality—only from 3% to 6%.

This result is not surprising. Inequality in the total population may be partitioned into inequality within the black and white populations and inequality between these two groups. Eliminating racial labor market discrimination against blacks will have no effect on inequality within the white population and little effect on inequality within the black population. Even if labor market discrimination has a large effect on inequality between the races, eliminating discrimination will have little effect on overall equality because whites constitute nearly 90% of the total population and inequality within the white population is nearly as large as inequality in the total population.

Although labor market discrimination against blacks does not account for a significant portion of total inequality in the United States, it does account for a significant portion of the inequality between the races. As our estimates in the third section of this chapter indicate, labor market discrimination accounts for from 43% to 60% of the racial earnings gap for males and from 30% to 39% of the racial earnings gap for families.

Conclusions

This chapter treats racial differences in economic status. In the first part of the chapter, we examine the degree to which comparisons of the relative well-being of blacks and whites are affected by different measures of economic status. In the second part, we examine the extent to which the labor market discrimination accounts for both the gap between the incomes of whites and blacks and overall inequality in the United States. In addition, we test the hypothesis that labor market discrimination is more severe against high-income blacks than against low-income blacks. Several findings stand out:

• The ratio of black to white net earnings capacity is smaller than the ratio of black to white earnings. Thus, if net earnings capacity is the preferred indicator of economic status, the black–white earnings ratio understates the actual disparity between the races in economic well-being.

• The black–white family net earnings capacity ratios increase monotonically over the entire distribution of earnings capacity. This suggests that racial differences in net earnings capacity are more serious at the bottom of the distribution than at the top.

• The black–white ratios of incomes, earnings, and earnings capacity are higher for men than for families. Thus, comparisons that focus only on racial differences in male earnings understate racial differences in family well-being.

• Although labor market discrimination accounts for a small portion—from 3% to 6%—of overall inequality in the United States, it accounts for from 43% to 60% of the total earnings gap between black and white males. If labor market discrimination were eliminated, the earnings of black men would increase by 25% to 35%.

• The severity of labor market discrimination against black men does not increase with earnings capacity when severity of discrimination is measured by the percentage increase in earnings that would result from the elimination of discrimination. In fact, our lower bound estimates suggest the opposite for both males and females. Our upper bound estimates for males suggest that severity of labor market discrimination is not systematically related to earnings capacity.

7

Earnings Capacity and
Economic Status: Summary

Most efforts since 1965 to develop a more satisfactory indicator of economic status have sought to expand the standard measure based on money income by incorporating aspects of economic welfare not captured in income flows. These aspects have included leisure time, in-kind transfers, intrafamily transfers, the annuitized value of wealth, and taxes. In this study, we approach the issue of economic status from a quite different peispective. Our analysis is based on the proposition that, at any point in time, the economic status of a living unit is accurately reflected in its economic capability—its capacity to generate a flow of income.

A Summary and Some Policy Implications

In Chapter 1, we briefly trace the line of development on which our work builds. The early contributions in this area were conceptual and associated primarily with the work of Friedman (1957), Ando and Modigliani (1963), and Duesenberry (1949); more recent work has been largely empirical. These later studies have been concentrated at the Survey Research Center at the University of Michigan and at the Institute for Research on Poverty at the University of Wisconsin (Moon and Smolensky 1977). Our work follows directly from the early conceptual studies in seeking a measure of economic status that is both independent of tastes for leisure and work and free of transitory effects. However, our study is primarily empirical and contributes only modestly to existing theoretical work. Hence it also builds on recent empirical efforts in this area, even though it proceeds by defining an indicator of economic status based on earnings capacity rather than by seeking to increase the comprehensiveness of the standard indicator.

In Chapter 2, we empirically define the concept of earnings capacity and describe the procedure and the data we employ in estimating the earnings capacity of a sample of American families. The primary aspect of this definition is the presumption that a living unit is performing at its capacity when the family head and the spouse (if present) are each employed 2000 hours per year at a wage rate that is representative of that earned by individuals with similar human capital and demographic characteristics.

The annual earnings such activity would yield are imputed to each individual in the sample by means of an earnings function fitted to the data by multiple regression analysis. The estimated earnings capacity for a family is obtained by summing this value[1] for the household head and spouse, adding to this sum interest, dividends, rent, and a few other kinds of unearned income as an estimate of capacity returns on physical capital, and adjusting the result for exogenously imposed limitations on work effort attributable to ill health and unemployment. This definition of earnings capacity is supplemented by an alternative definition that reflects the costs of attaining capacity work effort—primarily child care costs. The first measure we call *gross* earnings capacity; the second, *net* earnings capacity.

After estimating these capacity-based measures of economic status for each family in the survey, we analyze a number of relevant economic phenomena that the estimates illuminate. In Chapter 3, the

---

[1] For some of the analyses, this value is adjusted by means of a randomizing technique designed to replace some of the variance artificially eliminated in the regression-based imputations.

relationship of actual earnings to capacity earnings is estimated for each family, for various economic groups, and for the entire population. For the nonaged population—the groups for which the notion of capacity utilization is most relevant—we find that the rate of capacity utilization is about two-thirds if no value is attributed to services in the home produced by spouses and nearly three-fourths if such attribution is made. While the rate of capacity utilization is significantly higher for men than for women, virtually no difference is found between the rates of blacks and whites. Indeed, blacks of a given economic status, by and large, have slightly higher utilization rates than do whites of similar economic status. Also, families of low economic status are found to utilize their capacity at about the same rate as high-status families.

Clearly, differences in work effort among households contribute to observed inequality in the distribution of income. Because estimates of capacity utilization provide an indicator of household work effort, the extent of the contribution of this phenomenon to income inequality is also estimated in Chapter 3. Comparing the distributions of earnings capacity and pretransfer income, we conclude that at least 80% of the variation in income is caused by factors other than differences in capacity utilization.

Based on the findings of Chapter 3, we conclude that those who are poor by the income measure are not in that state because of relative failure on their part to exploit economic capacities. This suggests that neither laziness nor reliance upon public income transfers is responsible for low earnings. To the extent that public income transfer policy is shaped by the belief that the poor do not exploit their capacities—that they are "undeserving"—these findings may ultimately help to reshape such policy.

Chapter 4 employs the concept of earnings capacity to develop a definition of poverty based on the capabilities of households rather than on money income. Applying this definition to the estimates of household earnings capacity, we identify the composition of the earnings capacity poor and compare it with that of the poor as officially defined. We find that blacks, those who live in large families, and those who live in families with strong attachments to the labor market are more likely to be poor by the capacity-based definition than by the standard definition. The last finding suggests that the inadequate coverage of the working poor provided by our current income maintenance programs may be even less justifiable than evaluations that define poverty on the basis of current income have suggested. We also find that families headed by women are just as likely to be poor in terms of earnings capacity as in terms of current income. Thus, even if female heads of families worked at full-time, full-year jobs, they would need support from public income maintenance programs to lift them out of poverty.

Numerous income transfer programs—ranging from the negative income tax to earnings supplements to children's allowances—have been designed to reduce poverty. Because most of these measures are conditioned on income they target their benefits on the income poor. They tend to be less effective in assisting the earnings capacity poor. In Chapter 5, we demonstrate how the target efficiency of 10 income support programs is altered when the definition of poverty is shifted from the standard income-based definition to one based on earnings capacity. We find that the differences among programs in target efficiency are significantly changed when earnings capacity rather than current income is used as the measure of economic status. These results further call into question the usefulness of the criterion of target efficiency based on money income for evaluating income transfer programs.

Finally, the concept of earnings capacity is used in Chapter 6 to evaluate the contribution of labor market discrimination to black–white earnings differences. The estimates presented in that chapter lead to several conclusions. If economic status is presumed to be better reflected in earnings capacity than in current income, the disparity between blacks and whites is even greater than income differences imply. What is perhaps more serious, the disparity in status between blacks and whites is greater for low-capacity families than for high-capacity families. This disparity between the races is caused in large measure by discrimination against blacks in labor markets: Between 43% and 60% of the gap for men and between 30% and 39% of the gap for families is attributable to such discrimination. We conclude that policies designed to reduce labor market discrimination should play a prominent role in the overall effort to reduce racial differences in income. We also examine the degree to which the severity of labor market discrimination varies with earnings capacity and find no clear-cut pattern. Thus, there is no justification for focusing antidiscrimination policy on a particular part of the distribution of earnings capacity.

A Look Back and a Look Ahead

In developing the concept of earnings capacity and applying it to a number of important policy issues, we have accomplished several objectives. A new concept of household economic status which avoids several of the shortcomings of the traditional current income measure has been defined and evaluated. More important, this earnings capacity concept has been estimated empirically for each living unit in a large nationally weighted household sample and used in analyses of poverty and income distribution policies. When earnings capacity estimates are substituted for the current income measure in answering questions about poverty and income distribution, the bases for several widely accepted beliefs are severely challenged.

The composition of the households at the bottom of the distribution of economic status—the poor—is observed to be different from what has been indicated in a decade of published reports. The presumed superiority of certain income transfer programs in targeting benefits on those at the bottom of the distribution of economic status tends to evaporate when earnings capacity is substituted for income in defining economic status. While many suspect that poor people and blacks fail to take as much advantage of economic opportunities and capabilities as whites and those of high economic status, our results show that this is not the case. Families of low economic status and black families utilize as much of their earnings capacity as do rich and white households. In the same vein, we have shown that the high degree of income inequality in the United States stems primarily from inequalities in earnings capacity and not from the degree to which this capacity is exploited. Finally, using the earnings capacity concept, we presented additional evidence that a substantial portion of the difference between the earnings of blacks and those of whites is attributable to labor market discrimination against blacks.

Although these results demonstrate the merits of the earnings capacity concept and (we believe) justify our efforts to estimate and apply it, several improvements in both the concept and its estimation can be made. Some of these reflect aspects we would approach differently if we were now beginning the study. Others reflect the availability of new and more comprehensive microdata. With any large empirical study such as this, numerous choices are made and procedures are adopted that, with the advantage of hindsight, can be questioned.

First, for the majority of our analyses, we chose a data base with a large number of observations in order to maximize our ability to make comparisons across the distribution and among subgroups of the population. The cost of this was less extensive information on individual characteristics and a sacrifice in the variance of the earnings variable explained. Because of the troublesome problem of unmeasured characteristics and residual variation, use of a smaller but more detailed survey with more explanatory power but fewer possibilities for comparison might have been warranted.

Second, the specification of the earnings function was guided primarily by a human capital perspective and focused largely on the supply of labor. Perhaps more attention should have been paid to demand conditions confronted by individuals in the labor market.[2]

Third, given the problems of income underreporting and the neglect of intrafamily and public in-kind transfers in the survey, perhaps more effort should have been made to correct and supplement the data file.[3]

Fourth, both the adjustment for health and unemployment and the estimates of child care cost are but rough approximations. It is likely that independent supplementary studies based on alternative data sets could have improved on these estimates.[4] Similarly, supplementary studies could perhaps have produced improved estimates of the capacity return from assets other than human capital.

Fifth, our definition of earnings capacity is but one of a multitude of possible definitions. While all definitions require some degree of arbitrariness and researcher judgment, it would have been useful to have systematically tested the sensitivity of our estimates to alternatives that would bound the range of reasonable definitions.

As we have emphasized, a basic purpose of this study was to put forth the case for a concept of earnings capacity as an indicator of economic status and to make a first effort to give the concept some

[2] The importance of both the supply and demand sides of the market in explaining earnings has been emphasized in the work of Jan Tinbergen (1975).

[3] The importance of such efforts is emphasized by Smeeding (1975).

[4] In the case of health and unemployment, additional study perhaps could improve on the separation of permanent effects from temporary or taste-related effects. Additional work on the costs of engaging in work would have improved on the estimates of child care costs and would have included other components of such costs.

empirical basis. If the potential of the earnings capacity concept for measuring economic status and improving the evaluation of policy measures is accepted, the improvement of estimates of earnings capacity forms the agenda for the next round of research.

In addition to the economic phenomena and policy issues to which we have applied the concept of earnings capacity, the concept is relevant to a range of additional questions: evaluation of the role of labor market discrimination in accounting for earnings differences between men and women; the effect of guaranteed full employment on the size and utilization of the nation's earnings capacity; and the potential of supported work (or sheltered workshops) for increasing the level and use of earnings capacity by workers who are handicapped, low in skill, or disabled.

Moreover, the concept of earnings capacity again raises the possibility of developing a measure of economic position based on difficult-to-alter characteristics, a measure on which to focus tax and transfer policies. As the effects of existing policies on incentives to supply labor, invest in human capital, migrate, or alter family size and structure become of increasing concern, the advantage of such a "permanent" measure appears greater. The difficulties of developing such a reliable and acceptable indicator, however, should not be minimized.[5]

Finally, the concept of earnings capacity is important in organizing the evaluation of policies designed to reduce poverty and inequality. There are basically two ways to reduce inequality in earnings capacity: (a) reduce inequality in the distribution of human capital; or (b) reduce inequality in the distribution of market rewards for the use of human capital. In addition, poverty and inequality caused by low earnings capacity can be offset by income maintenance programs. Although there have been numerous studies of existing and proposed income maintenance programs and numerous studies of the effectiveness of education and training programs designed to reduce human inequalities in human capital and earnings capacity, far fewer studies have focused on the effectiveness of policies designed to alter the pattern of market rewards for a given distribution of human capital. Increasingly, measures with this objective are being debated in Western democracies. Such strategies include equal opportunity policies designed to reduce race and sex discrimination, corporate

[5] This potentiality has also been emphasized by Tinbergen (see Haveman 1977).

policies that seek to narrow wage gaps within the enterprise (motivated, in large part, by trade unions and the public sector), schemes designed to concentrate employment demands for both public and private activities (for example, public works) on low-skill, high-unemployment occupations, dynamic minimum wage policies designed to reduce the ratio of the median to the minimum wage over time, plans to increase the participation of workers in decisions previously reserved to management (for example, the wage structure, the capital and skill intensity of new investments, and the allocation of profits between labor and capital owners), public employment schemes, and wage or earnings supplements. The concept of earnings capacity is basic in evaluating this menu of options to alter the pattern of market rewards. It is also basic in evaluating the cost of reducing inequality by the strategy of altering market rewards versus the strategies of increasing income transfers or altering the distribution of earnings capacity. Systematically extending the application of the earnings capacity concept along these lines constitutes an ambitious research agenda.

Appendix A
Estimating Lorenz Curves and Gini Coefficients

In this appendix, the procedure employed in estimating the Lorenz curve and the Gini coefficient for each of the distributions of economic status is described (see Kakwani and Podder 1973).

Let $\pi(x)$ be the proportion of the total family units having income or earnings capacity less than x dollars, and let $\eta(x)$ be the proportion of total income held by these family units. The Lorenz curve, then, is the graphical representation of the relationship between the two variables π and η. If we had knowledge of the law governing the generation of income in the population, the Lorenz curve could in principle be mathematically determined from this law. But without knowledge of the underlying income-generating law, a functional relationship for the Lorenz curve can be obtained solely on a goodness-of-fit criterion. This procedure is followed in this book.

In general, the Lorenz curve must meet the following four conditions:

1. if $\pi = 0 \gtreqless \eta = 0$;
2. if $\pi = 1 \gtreqless \eta = 1$;
3. $\eta < \pi$;

4. the slope of the curve increases monotonically, that is, $\delta^2\eta/\delta\pi^2 > 0$.

Kakwani and Podder have suggested the following functional form for the Lorenz curve, which satisfies these four conditions:

$$\eta = \pi e - \beta(1 - \pi). \tag{A.1}$$

While this function is nonlinear in π, it is linear in the parameter, β. Thus, a straightforward transformation of equation (A.1) allows us to estimate β from the regression of $\ln(\pi/\eta)$ on $(1 - \pi)$.

The Gini coefficient is defined to be equal to twice the area between the Lorenz curve and the 45° line. Thus the Gini coefficient implied by equation (A.1) is equal to

$$\text{Gini} = 2\,(1/2 - \int_0^1 \pi\, e^{-\beta(1-\pi)}\, d\pi)$$

$$= 1 - [2(\beta - 1)/\beta^2] - (2e^{-\beta}/\beta^2). \tag{A.2}$$

Hence, once we have estimated β from the data, the Gini coefficient can be directly calculated from equation (A.2).

Appendix *B*
Effect of Randomization on
Estimates of Earnings Capacity

As emphasized in the text, the CY and EC comparisons of the composition of the poverty population (Table 4.1) employ EC estimates based on the randomization procedures described in Chapter 2. Two questions arise regarding the reliability of these results. First, to what extent are the comparisons dependent on the application of the randomization adjustment? Second, to what extent are the EC estimates and, hence, the comparisons artifacts of the particular constellation of random impacts produced by the procedure: That is, to what extent are the EC estimates a chance happening? In an attempt to answer these questions, we present in Table B.1 two additional sets of data on the composition of the poor population. The first new set of estimates, labeled $\widetilde{NEC}_1^*$, differs from the $\widetilde{NEC}^*$ estimates (Table 4.1) only in that a second random number generator process was employed in obtaining it. The second new set of estimates, labeled NEC^*, employs the same earnings functions as those used in developing the $\widetilde{NEC}^*$ estimates but assigns the expected value of earnings capacity rather than the expected value plus or minus a random shock. For purposes of comparison, Table B.1 also

101

RANDOMIZED AND NONRANDOMIZED DISTRIBUTIONS OF
EARNINGS CAPACITY AND CURRENT INCOME POOR INDIVIDUALS,
BY SOCIOECONOMIC CHARACTERISTICS: TOTAL POPULATION

	$\widetilde{NEC}^*$	$\widetilde{NEC}_1^*$	NEC^*	Current income
Race of head				
White	59.96	61.31	52.05	67.70
Black	38.34	37.47	46.24	30.82
Other	1.70	1.22	1.71	1.33
Sex of head				
Male	49.88	49.83	47.29	45.60
Female	50.12	50.17	52.71	54.40
Age of head				
16–21	2.38	2.64	2.43	4.69
22–30	21.53	23.08	20.02	17.07
31–40	29.47	28.35	27.74	22.62
41–50	19.93	19.41	19.34	17.37
51–60	10.92	11.38	12.58	12.66
61–64	2.80	2.62	2.98	4.70
65 or more	12.96	12.43	14.90	20.87
Family size				
1	6.25	6.42	4.26	19.29
2	6.26	6.61	5.25	14.64
3–4	22.94	23.12	20.71	22.06
5–6	28.35	28.91	28.34	20.54
7–8	21.16	20.35	23.06	15.25
9 or more	15.24	14.59	18.37	8.22
Education of head				
0–8	46.71	45.26	55.84	48.94
9–12	47.76	48.43	41.54	41.65
13–16	5.23	6.08	2.59	8.36
17 or more	.31	.23	0	1.06
Occupation of head				
Professional	3.60	3.92	2.07	3.44
Farmer	2.95	2.79	2.86	12.84
Manager	5.12	5.52	3.08	8.15
Clerical	9.53	9.91	8.05	5.13
Sales	2.59	2.80	1.84	2.96
Craftsman	13.70	14.22	12.19	9.60
Operative	26.57	26.32	28.15	16.97
Private household	5.13	5.26	5.78	8.66
Service	15.68	15.48	17.26	17.34
Farm laborer	5.21	5.02	6.53	6.53
Laborer	9.90	8.77	12.19	9.33

Table B.1   (Continued)

	$\widetilde{NEC}^*$	$\widetilde{NEC}_1^*$	NEC^*	Current income
Region				
Northeast	17.41	17.86	15.84	15.72
North Central	21.49	22.14	18.80	22.61
South	46.44	45.90	52.22	46.24
West	14.66	14.10	13.14	15.42
Location				
Town	15.92	15.30	16.22	13.99
Rural	34.47	35.44	38.48	40.58
Suburb	15.84	16.24	12.16	14.44
Central city	33.77	33.02	33.14	30.99
Number of earners				
0	27.28	27.28	30.84	42.18
1	52.63	54.07	51.6	45.02
2	20.09	18.65	17.56	12.81
Weeks worked (head)				
0	28.34	28.59	32.30	43.65
1–13	7.43	7.46	8.21	9.58
14–26	7.68	6.98	9.12	7.99
27–39	7.82	8.66	9.82	6.58
40–47	6.40	5.60	5.93	4.58
48–49	2.87	2.98	2.68	1.70
50–52	39.45	39.74	31.14	25.92
Work (head)				
Full time	83.44	84.41	80.31	73.44
Part time	16.56	15.59	19.69	26.56

NOTE: Values are expressed in percentages.

reproduces both the CY figures and the $\widetilde{NEC}^*$ figures from Table 4.1.

In comparing the two sets of randomized estimates ($\widetilde{NEC}^*$ and $\widetilde{NEC}_1^*$, we see that the differences are exceedingly small. Of the 53 pairs of numbers that can be compared in these two columns, the elements of no pair differ by as much as 2 percentage points, and the elements of only 7 pairs differ by between 1 and 2 percentage points. From this, we conclude that the particular set of randomized estimates used in Table 4.1 does not account for the comparisons of the composition of the EC poor with that of the CY poor. Substituting $\widetilde{NEC}_1^*$ for $\widetilde{NEC}^*$ would require no change in the discussion or the conclusions.

As expected, some nontrivial differences exist between the composition of the EC poor estimated by the random and the nonrandom procedures. Most of the differences, however, are small. In most cases, the randomization procedure reduces the difference between the composition of the EC poor and that of the CY poor. Hence the differences between the composition of the $\widetilde{NEC}^*$ poor and that of the CY poor in terms of race, years of schooling, region, and family size are smaller than the differences between the compositions of the NEC^* poor and the CY poor. Recall that the nonrandomized estimates assign the cell mean to each family unit within a cell defined by race, age, location, sex, and years of schooling. This procedure artificially suppresses the variance among observations within a cell. As a result, the importance of these explanatory variables is exaggerated. This procedure, for example, assigns *all* black female heads with fewer than 12 years of schooling to the bottom part of the income distribution. It was to avoid this artificial elimination of variance within cells that the randomization procedure was adopted.

In two cases, however, the differences between the $\widetilde{NEC}^*$ poor and the CY poor are larger than the differences between the NEC^* poor and the CY poor. Even in these cases, however, the differences between the NEC^* composition and the CY composition are notable. The proportion of the poor who live in households with no earners is 42% for the CY definition, 27% for $\widetilde{NEC}^*$, and 31% for NEC^*. The proportion of poor individuals who live in households with aged heads is 21% for CY, 13% for $\widetilde{NEC}^*$, and 15% for NEC^*. The larger percentage of aged poor in the nonrandomized estimates is attributable to the negative effect of randomization on the proportion of the poor who have earners in their households. In the absence of this effect, we would expect the proportion of the aged to be closer to the CY proportion in the randomized estimates than in the nonrandomized estimates, as is the case for other variables in the regression.

In conclusion, two points should be emphasized. First, the contrast between the composition of the EC poor and the CY poor is not attributable to the randomization technique used in this study. Second, because the nonrandomized estimates are based on a procedure that artificially eliminates any within-cell variance, the randomized estimates are, for most purposes, superior. Consequently, except where explicitly noted, only the randomized EC estimates are used in the discussion in the text.

Appendix **C**

Composition of the Earnings Capacity and Current Income Poor in the Nonaged Population

The estimates presented in Table 4.1 indicated that heads of EC poor families tend to work substantially more than heads of CY poor families. The table also emphasized that a substantially higher proportion of the CY poor than of the EC poor live in households headed by aged persons. These two differences are obviously related. The analysis in this appendix is confined to the nonaged population. The objective is to ascertain the extent to which the differences in the composition of EC and CY poverty observed in Table 4.1 are attributable to the special characteristics of the aged.

In 1973, 9.9% of the population age 64 or younger lived in families classified as poor by the official CY definition of poverty. This is to be compared to 11% of the total population living in families so classified. Data on the composition of these nonaged CY poor are presented in Table C.1 along with data on the composition of the nonaged EC poor, that is, the bottom 9.9% of the $\widetilde{GEC}^*$ and $\widetilde{NEC}^*$ distributions of the nonaged population. These data can be compared to those in the first three columns of Table 4.1 to isolate the effect of the aged on the composition of the poor.

In general, the effect on the composition of the poor of moving

Table C.1

DISTRIBUTION OF EARNINGS CAPACITY AND CURRENT INCOME
POOR INDIVIDUALS, BY SOCIOECONOMIC CHARACTERISTICS:
NONAGED POPULATION

	$\widetilde{NEC}$*	$\widetilde{GEC}$*	Current income
Race of head			
White	57.69	57.72	64.9
Black	40.59	40.39	33.54
Other	1.71	1.89	1.56
Sex of head			
Male	50.45	42.18	55.74
Female	49.55	57.82	44.26
Age of head			
16–21	2.86	3.01	5.92
22–30	25.51	18.34	21.58
31–40	33.46	28.23	28.61
41–50	21.66	25.80	21.95
51–60	12.34	18.90	16.00
61–64	3.16	5.73	5.94
Family size			
1	2.43	7.49	11.17
2	4.18	7.65	10.18
3–4	23.41	24.60	25.35
5–6	29.98	27.34	24.73
7–8	22.48	20.33	18.55
9 or more	17.53	12.58	10.01
Education of head			
0–8	41.19	43.49	42.66
9–12	52.90	50.04	47.15
13–16	5.59	6.04	9.14
17 or more	.33	.42	1.05
Occupation of head			
Professional	3.93	3.91	3.37
Farmer	2.11	1.72	11.95
Manager	5.10	4.79	8.06
Clerical	9.98	13.04	5.14
Sales	2.64	2.64	2.88
Craftsman	13.81	11.96	10.00
Operative	27.34	25.75	17.91
Private household	4.97	5.74	6.15
Service	16.01	17.77	15.61
Farm laborer	5.28	4.49	7.79
Laborer	8.83	8.19	11.13

Table C.1   (Continued)

	$\widetilde{NEC}^*$	$\widetilde{GEC}^*$	Current income
Region			
Northeast	16.54	17.34	14.93
North Central	21.38	20.70	21.81
South	46.28	46.03	46.41
West	15.81	15.84	16.85
Location			
Town	15.58	16.04	13.01
Rural	35.71	36.29	40.40
Suburb	15.19	14.81	14.71
Central city	33.52	32.86	31.88
Number of earners			
0	21.28	21.88	31.95
1	56.97	58.32	52.94
2	21.75	19.80	15.11
Weeks worked (head)			
0	21.98	22.89	33.21
1–13	8.09	8.56	10.90
14–26	8.11	8.85	9.38
27–39	8.64	8.89	8.02
40–47	7.07	6.71	5.57
48–49	3.32	2.45	2.10
50–52	42.79	41.65	30.81
Work (head)			
Full time	84.90	83.58	76.06
Part time	15.10	16.42	23.94

NOTE: Values are expressed in percentages.

from the *CY* to the *EC* definition is not greatly different for the nonaged population than for the total population. Again, the *EC* poor population has more blacks, more large families, fewer family heads with higher education, fewer rural residents, fewer farmers, and more adults with high work effort than does the *CY* poor population. The most prominent difference in pattern between the two definitions of poverty comes in the composition of the poor by sex of head. For the total population (Table 4.1), the *CY* definition shows 54% and the *NEC* definition about 50% of the poor population living in families headed by women. For the nonaged population, the proportion of the *NEC* poor living in families headed by women remains at about 50%

while the proportion of the *CY* poor living in such families is only 44%.

However, considering the nonaged population rather than the total population does result in substantial differences in the composition of the poor population by both definitions of poverty. First, a far higher proportion of the poor in the nonaged population live in families with one or two workers. In the total population, about 73% of the *NEC* poor and 58% of the *CY* poor live in such families; the comparable figures for the nonaged population are 79% and 68%. Similar differences between the two populations are observed in the data on weeks worked and on full-time versus part-time work. Second, blacks make up an even higher proportion of the nonaged poor population (41% for *NEC*, 34% for *CY*) than of the total poor population (38% for *NEC*, 31% for *CY*). Third, not unexpectedly, a substantially smaller proportion of the nonaged poor live in families of two or fewer persons.

Finally, it should be noted that the differences between the *NEC* and *GEC* figures tend to be smaller for the nonaged population. Because the aged have few children, the child care deduction that distinguishes *GEC* from *NEC* has a more powerful effect on the ranking of families in the total population than in the nonaged population. As noted earlier, this change in relative ranking accounts for a significant part of the difference between the *NEC* and *GEC* distributions. Confining the analysis to the nonaged, therefore, leads to smaller compositional differences between *NEC* and *GEC*.

Appendix D
Earnings Functions from Michigan Income Dynamics Panel Study Data

CPS-STYLE EARNINGS FUNCTIONS FOR BLACK AND WHITE MEN AND WOMEN: MICHIGAN PANEL STUDY DATA

Independent variable	Men		Women	
	White coefficient	Black coefficient	White coefficient	Black coefficient
Northeast	.0618 (1.6)	.3167 (4.9)	.1440 (2.8)	.2761 (3.3)
North Central	.0909 (2.9)	.1858 (3.7)	.0602 (1.4)	.1022 (1.7)
West	.0115 (0.3)	.0836 (1.3)	.0220 (0.5)	.0953 (1.2)
SMSA1	.3173 (9.0)	.3295 (6.5)	.2359 (5.1)	.3981 (5.9)
SMSA2	.2571 (7.4)	.3004 (5.4)	.1910 (4.1)	.2592 (3.5)
SMSA3	.0979 (2.4)	.2310 (3.5)	−.0211 (0.4)	.1787 (2.1)
SMSA4	.1593 (3.1)	.0256 (0.3)	.0664 (0.9)	.1718 (1.5)
Age	.0809 (13.4)	.0657 (6.9)	.0487 (5.4)	.0357 (2.6)
Age^2	−.0010 (16.6)	−.0008 (8.3)	−.0005 (5.8)	−.0005 (3.5)
Education	−.0421 (2.7)	−.0461 (2.2)	−.0410 (1.6)	−.0464 (1.3)
Education^2	.0029 (5.2)	.0036 (4.1)	.0057 (6.6)	.0055 (4.4)
Education × age	.0008 (3.5)	.0005 (1.5)	−.0003 (0.8)	.0002 (0.3)
Hours	.0019 (34.6)	.0022 (27.8)	.0026 (46.0)	.0026 (29.1)
Hours^2	$-.3 \times 10^{-6}$ (27.6)	$-.4 \times 10^{-6}$ (20.9)	$-.5 \times 10^{-6}$ (26.0)	$-.5 \times 10^{-6}$ (17.0)
Not married, no children			.0477 (0.9)	−.0200 (0.3)
Not married, with children			−.0798 (1.3)	−.0920 (1.8)
Married, no children			.0787 (1.9)	.0129 (0.2)
Constant	4.5286 (24.7)	4.3472 (17.8)	3.9747 (14.7)	4.1630 (11.0)
r^2	.61	.65	.76	.72
F	257	124	307	143

NOTE: t values appear in parentheses.

Table D.2

FULL EARNINGS FUNCTIONS FOR BLACK AND WHITE MEN:
MICHIGAN PANEL STUDY DATA

Independent variable	White coefficient		Black coefficient	
Northeast	.0250	(0.6)	.2767	(4.3)
North Central	.0745	(2.3)	.1445	(2.8)
West	−.0066	(0.2)	.0842	(1.3)
SMSA1	.3072	(8.7)	.3195	(6.2)
SMSA2	.2502	(7.3)	.3085	(5.5)
SMSA3	.0920	(2.2)	.2301	(3.5)
SMSA4	.1438	(2.8)	.0361	(0.5)
Age	.0838	(10.7)	.0780	(5.5)
Age^2	−.0010	(12.3)	−.0010	(6.2)
Education	−.0660	(3.3)	−.0531	(2.3)
Education^2	.0027	(4.5)	.0025	(2.7)
Education × age	.0009	(3.8)	.0006	(1.7)
Hours	.0019	(34.4)	.0022	(27.2)
Hours^2	$-.3 \times 10^{-6}$	(27.5)	$-.4 \times 10^{-6}$	(20.7)
Major disfigurement	−.3752	(3.2)	−.1657	(1.4)
Minor disfigurement	−.2000	(3.1)	−.1765	(1.9)
Major language problem	−.0652	(0.6)	.1772	(1.1)
Minor language problem	.0122	(0.2)	.0511	(0.7)
IQ	.0038	(0.2)	.0114	(0.8)
IQ × Education	.0015	(1.1)	.0018	(1.2)
Training	.0852	(3.0)	.0230	(0.5)
School expenditures	.0003	(2.4)	.0002	(1.1)
DUMSHX	.0005	(0.0)	.0766	(1.3)
Father's education	.0078	(2.2)	.0020	(0.4)
Father not poor	.0506	(1.9)	−.0773	(1.3)
Constant	4.3635	(15.8)	3.9848	(11.0)
r^2	.61		.66	
F	149		72	

NOTE: t values appear in parentheses.

Appendix E

Upper and Lower Bound Measures of the Role of Labor Market Discrimination

The upper and lower bound measures of the contribution of labor market discrimination to observed black–white earnings differentials can be stated formally as follows:

Let the earnings functions for blacks and whites be characterized as

$$E_W = \beta_W \mathbf{X}_W + \alpha_W \mathbf{H}_W \tag{E.1}$$

$$E_B = \beta_B \mathbf{X}_B + \alpha_B \mathbf{H}_B, \tag{E.2}$$

where E_W (E_B) is the earnings of whites (blacks), $\mathbf{X}_W$ ($\mathbf{X}_B$) is a vector of human capital characteristics describing whites (blacks), $\mathbf{H}_W$ ($\mathbf{H}_B$) is a vector of the hours worked per year of whites (blacks), β_W (β_B) is a vector of partial regression coefficients describing the relationship of changes in elements of $\mathbf{X}_W$ ($\mathbf{X}_B$) to changes in E_W (E_B), and α_W (α_B) is a vector of partial regression coefficients describing the relationship of changes in elements of $\mathbf{H}_W$ ($\mathbf{H}_B$) to changes in E_W (E_B). Assume that these relationships are perfectly specified with $r^2 = 1$.

Observing these relationships at the means of the dependent and independent variables, we can write

$$\bar{E}_W - \bar{E}_B = (\beta_W \bar{\mathbf{X}}_W + \alpha_W \bar{\mathbf{H}}_W) - (\beta_B \bar{\mathbf{X}}_B + \alpha_B \bar{\mathbf{H}}_B). \qquad \text{(E.3)}$$

Adding two zero terms, $(\beta_W \bar{\mathbf{X}}_B - \beta_W \bar{\mathbf{X}}_B)$ and $(\alpha_W \mathbf{H}_B - \alpha_W \mathbf{H}_B)$, to the right-hand side of equation (E.3), and collecting terms, we obtain

$$\bar{E}_W - \bar{E}_B = [\beta_W(\bar{\mathbf{X}}_W - \bar{\mathbf{X}}_B)] + [\alpha_W(\mathbf{H}_W - \bar{\mathbf{H}}_B)]$$
$$+ [\bar{\mathbf{X}}_B(\beta_W - \beta_B) + \bar{\mathbf{H}}_B(\alpha_W - \alpha_B)] \quad \text{(E.4)}$$

The last right-hand term of equation (E.4) can be rewritten as $(\beta_W \bar{\mathbf{X}}_B + \alpha_W \bar{\mathbf{H}}_B) - (\beta_B \bar{\mathbf{X}}_B + \alpha_B \bar{\mathbf{H}}_B)$ and, using the notation from the text, identified as

$$G^{LMD} = EC_B^W (\bar{\mathbf{H}}_B) - EC_B (\bar{\mathbf{H}}_B). \qquad \text{(E.5)}$$

The first term in equation (E.5) is the amount the black with mean human capital characteristics $(\bar{\mathbf{X}}_B)$ would earn if he worked the mean hours of blacks and if his human capital characteristics and his hours were valued in the market as white characteristics and hours are valued. The first and second terms on the right side of equation (E.5) are the amount the same black would earn if his characteristics and his hours were valued as black characteristics are valued. This is a lower bound estimate of the portion of $\bar{E}_W - \bar{E}_B$ accounted for by labor market discrimination, because it is the residual of $E_W - E_B$ after removal of (a) all differences between blacks and whites in human capital (valued as the market values white characteristics); and (b) all differences between blacks and whites in hours worked per year (valued as the market values white hours worked)—the first and second terms in the right-hand side of equation (E.4), respectively.

The upper bound estimate of the portion of $\bar{E}_W - \bar{E}_B$ accounted for by labor market discrimination (G_U^{LMD}) is obtained by attributing both the second and the third terms from the right-hand side of equation (E.4) to labor market discrimination. Hence, when only the first term from the right-hand side of equation (E.4) is removed from $\bar{E}_W - \bar{E}_B$, the residual includes both (G_L^{LMD}) and all differences between blacks and whites in hours worked per year (valued as the market values white hours worked). This residual is identified as the upper bound estimate of the portion of $\bar{E}_W - \bar{E}_B$ that is accounted for by labor market discrimination, because, in addition to (G_L^{LMD}) it attributes all differences between blacks and whites in hours worked to labor market discrimination. Rewriting the last two terms of equation (E.4)and then collecting terms, we obtain

$$(\beta_W \bar{\mathbf{X}}_B + \alpha_W \bar{\bar{\mathbf{H}}}_W) - (\beta_B \bar{\mathbf{X}}_B + \alpha_B \bar{\bar{\mathbf{H}}}_B), \tag{E.6}$$

which, using the notation from the text, is identified as the upper bound of the portion of $\bar{E}_W - \bar{E}_B$ accounted for by labor market discrimination:

$$G_U^{LMD} = EC_B^W (\bar{\bar{\mathbf{H}}}_W) - EC_B (\bar{\bar{\mathbf{H}}}_B). \tag{E.7}$$

References

Academic Computing Center. 1969. Random number routines. In *Reference manual for 1108*. Mimeographed. Madison: University of Wisconsin.

Ando, Albert, and Modigliani, Franco. 1963. The "life cycle" hypothesis of saving: aggregate implications and tests. *American Economic Review* 53:55–84.

Ashenfelter, Orley. 1970. Changes in labor market discrimination over time. *Journal of Human Resources* 5:403–430.

Atkinson, Anthony. 1970. On the measurement of inequality. *Journal of Economic Theory* 2:244–263.

Barth, Michael C., Carcagno, George J., and Palmer, John L. 1974. *Toward an effective income support system: problems, prospects, and choices.* Madison: University of Wisconsin, Institute for Research on Poverty.

Batchelder, Alan. 1964. Decline in the relative income of Negro men. *Quarterly Journal of Economics* 78:525–548.

Becker, Gary S. 1965. A theory of the allocation of time. *The Economic Journal* 75:493–517.

Beller, Andrea. 1974. The effects of Title VII of the Civil Rights Act of 1964 on the economic position of minorities. Ph.D. dissertation, Columbia University.

Blinder, Alan S. 1973. Wage discrimination: reduced form and structural estimates. *Journal of Human Resources* 8:436–455.

Blinder, Alan S. 1974. *Towards an economic theory of income distribution.* Cambridge: MIT Press.

Box, G. E. P., and Muller, M. E. 1958. A note on the generation of random normal deviates. *Annals of Mathematical Statistics* 28:610–611.

Bronfenbrenner, Martin. 1971. *Income distribution theory.* Chicago: Aldine–Atherton.

Christensen, Sandra, and Bernard, Keith. 1974. The black–white earnings gap. *Journal of Human Resources* 9:476–489.

David, Martin H. 1959. Welfare income and budget needs. *Review of Economics and Statistics* 41:393–399.

Duesenberry, James S. 1949. *Income, saving, and the theory of consumer behavior.* Cambridge: Harvard University Press.

Friedman, Milton. 1957. *A theory of the consumption function.* Princeton: Princeton University Press.

Galbraith, John Kenneth; Kuh, Edwin; and Thurow, Lester C. 1971. The Galbraith plan to promote the minorities. *New York Times Magazine,* Aug. 22, pp. 9+.

Garfinkel, Irwin, and Haveman, Robert. 1974. Earnings capacity and the target efficiency of alternative transfer programs. *American Economic Review* 64 (May 1974, Papers and Proceedings): 196–204.

Garfinkel, Irwin, and Haveman, Robert. 1977. Earnings capacity, economic status, and poverty. *Journal of Human Resources* 12:49–70.

Garfinkel, Irwin, and Kesselman, Jonathan R. 1976. *On the efficiency of income testing in tax-transfer programs.* Madison: University of Wisconsin, Institute for Research on Poverty, Discussion Paper 339–76.

Garfinkel, Irwin, and Masters, Stanley. 1978. *Estimating labor supply effects of income maintenance alternatives.* New York: Academic Press.

Guthrie, Harold. 1970. The prospect of equality between white and black families under varying rates of unemployment. *Journal of Human Resources* 5:431–448.

Gwartney, J. 1970. Discrimination and income differentials. *American Economic Review* 60:396–408.

Haveman, Robert. 1973. Work conditioned subsidies as an income maintenance strategy. In *Concepts in welfare program design,* U.S. Congress, Joint Economic Committee, *Studies in Public Welfare* no. 9, pp. 33–67. Washington, D.C.: U.S. Government Printing Office.

Haveman, Robert. 1977. Tinbergen's income distribution: analysis and policies—a review article. *Journal of Human Resources* 12:103–114.

Haveman, Robert; Lurie, Irene; and Mirer, Thad. 1974. Earnings supplementation plans for working poor families: an evaluation of alternatives. In *Benefit–cost and policy analysis—1973,* ed. Robert Haveman *et al.,* pp. 291–318. Chicago: Aldine.

Jencks, Christopher *et al.* 1972. *Inequality: a reassessment of the effect of family and schooling in America.* New York: Basic Books.

Kakwani, N. C., and Podder, N. 1973. On the estimation of Lorenz curves from grouped observations. *International Economic Review* 14:278–292.

Kiker, B. F., and Liles, W. Pierce. 1974. Earnings, employment and racial discrimination: additional evidence. *American Economic Review* 64:492–501.

Krashinsky, Michael. 1975. Day care and welfare. In *Integrating income maintenance programs,* ed. Irene Lurie, pp. 289–334. New York: Academic Press.

Lurie, Irene. 1974. Estimates of tax rates in the AFDC program. *National Tax Journal* 27:93–111.

Masters, Stanley. 1974. The effect of educational differences and labor market discrimination on the relative earnings of black males. *Journal of Human Resources* 9:342–360.

Masters, Stanley. 1975. *Black-white income differentials*. New York: Academic Press.

McClung, Nelson; Moeller, John; and Siguel, Eduardo. 1971. *Transfer income program evaluation*. Washington, D.C.: Urban Institute, Working Paper 950-3.

Miller, Herman. 1966. *Income distribution in the U.S.* A 1960 Census Monograph. Washington, D.C.: U.S. Government Printing Office.

Mincer, Jacob. 1974. *Education, experience, and earnings*. New York: National Bureau of Economic Research.

Moon, Marilyn L. 1977. *The measurement of economic welfare*. New York: Academic Press.

Moon, Marilyn L., and Smolensky, Eugene, eds. 1977. *Improving measures of economic well-being*. New York: Academic Press.

Morgan, James N. 1968. The supply of effort, the measurement of well-being, and the dynamics of improvement. *American Economic Review* 58 (May 1968, Papers and Proceedings): 31–39.

Morgan, James N. *et al.* 1962. *Income and welfare in the United States*. New York: McGraw-Hill.

Morgan, James N.; Sirageldin, Ismail; and Baerwaldt, Nancy. 1965. *Productive Americans*. Ann Arbor: University of Michigan, Survey Research Center.

Morgan, James N., and Smith, James D. 1969. Measures of economic well-offness and their correlates. *American Economic Review* 59:450–462.

Morgan, James N. *et al.* 1974. *Five thousand American families: patterns of economic progress*. 2 vols. Ann Arbor: University of Michigan, Institute for Social Research.

Nicholson, J. L. 1976. Appraisal of different methods of estimating equivalence scales and their results. *Review of Income and Wealth* 22:1–11.

Orshansky, Molly. 1965. Counting the poor: another look at the poverty people. *Social Security Bulletin* 28:3–29.

Pechman, Joseph A., and Okner, Benjamin A. 1975. *Who bears the tax burden?* Washington, D.C.: The Brookings Institution.

Projector, Dorothy, and Bretz, Judith. 1975. Measurement of transfer income in the Current Population Survey. In *The personal distribution of income and wealth*, ed. James D. Smith, pp. 377–448. New York: National Bureau of Economic Research.

Projector, Dorothy S., and Weiss, Gertrude S. 1969. Income–net worth measures of economic welfare. *Social Security Bulletin* 32:14–17.

Reynolds, Morgan O., and Brown, William W. 1974. Discrimination and the residual approach. Unpublished.

Schmundt, Maria; Smolensky, Eugene; and Stiefel, Leanna. 1975. When do recipients value in-kind transfers at their cost to taxpayers? In *Integrating income maintenance programs*, ed. Irene Lurie, pp. 189–207. New York: Academic Press.

Schultz, T. Paul. 1965. *The distribution of personal income*. U.S. Congress, Joint Economic Committee, Subcommittee on Economic Statistics. Washington, D.C.: U.S. Government Printing Office.

Seneca, Joseph J., and Taussig, Michael K. 1971. Family equivalence scales and personal income tax exemptions for children. *Review of Economics and Statistics* 53:253–262.

Sirageldin, Ismail. 1969. Non-market components of national income. Ann Arbor: University of Michigan, Survey Research Center.

Smeeding, Timothy. 1975. Measuring the economic welfare of low income households and the antipoverty effectiveness of cash transfer programs. Ph.D. dissertation, University of Wisconsin.

Smith, James D., and Morgan, James N. 1970. Variability of economic well-being and its determinants. *American Economic Review* 60:286–295.

Taussig, Michael K. 1973. *Alternative measures of the distribution of economic welfare.* Princeton: Princeton University, Industrial Relations Section.

Thurow, Lester C. 1975. *Generating inequality.* New York: Basic Books.

Tinbergen, Jan. 1975. *Income distribution: analysis and policies.* Amsterdam: North-Holland.

U.S. Bureau of the Census. 1971. *The social and economic status of Negroes in the United States.* Current Population Survey, Series P-23, Special Studies no. 38. Washington, D.C.: U.S. Government Printing Office.

U.S. Bureau of the Census. 1973. *Money income in 1972 of families and persons in the United States.* Current Population Survey, Series P-60, no. 90. Washington, D.C.: U.S. Government Printing Office.

Vroman, Wayne. 1974. Changes in black workers' relative earnings: evidence from the 1960's. In *Patterns of racial discrimination,* ed. George von Furstenberg et al., vol. 2:169–196. Lexington, Mass.: D.C. Heath.

Watts, Harold W., and Cain, Glen C. 1971. *Income maintenance and labor supply.* New York: Academic Press.

Weisbrod, Burton. 1969. Collective action and the distribution of income: a conceptual approach. In *The analysis and evaluation of public expenditures, the PPB system,* U.S. Congress, Joint Economic Committee, pp. 177–200. Washington, D.C.: U.S. Government Printing Office.

Weisbrod, Burton, and Hansen, W. Lee. 1968. An income–net worth approach to measuring economic welfare. *American Economic Review* 58:1315–1329.

Wohlstetter, Albert, and Coleman, Sinclair. 1970. *Race differences in income.* Santa Monica: Rand Corporation.

Institute for Research on Poverty
Monograph Series

Vernon L. Allen, Editor, *Psychological Factors in Poverty*

Frederick Williams, Editor, *Language and Poverty: Perspectives on a Theme*

Murray Edelman, *Politics as Symbolic Action: Mass Arousal and Quiescence*

Joel F. Handler and Ellen Jane Hollingsworth, *"The Deserving Poor": A Study of Welfare Administration*

Robert J. Lampman, *Ends and Means of Reducing Income Poverty*

Larry L. Orr, Robinson G. Hollister, and Myron J. Lefcowitz, Editors, with the assistance of Karen Hester, *Income Maintenance: Interdisciplinary Approaches to Research*

Charles E. Metcalf, *An Econometric Model of the Income Distribution*

Glen G. Cain and Harold W. Watts, Editors, *Income Maintenance and Labor Supply: Econometric Studies*

Joel F. Handler, *The Coercive Social Worker: British Lessons for American Social Services*

Larry L. Orr, *Income, Employment, and Urban Residential Location*

Stanley H. Masters, *Black–White Income Differentials: Empirical Studies and Policy Implications*

Irene Lurie, Editor, *Integrating Income Maintenance Programs*

Peter K. Eisinger, *Patterns of Interracial Politics: Conflict and Cooperation in the City*

David Kershaw and Jerilyn Fair, *The New Jersey Income-Maintenance Experiment, Volume I: Operations, Surveys, and Administration*

Fredrick L. Golladay and Robert H. Haveman, *The Economic Impacts of Tax–Transfer Policy: Regional and Distributional Effects*

Morgan Reynolds and Eugene Smolensky, *Public Expenditures, Taxes, and the Distribution of Income: The United States, 1950, 1961, 1970*